THE LAST FLIGHTS OF MALAYSIAN AIRLINES MH370 AND MH17
A Firsthand-Look

THE LAST FLIGHTS OF MALAYSIAN AIRLINES MH370 AND MH17
A Firsthand-Look

Azharuddin Abdul Rahman
Department Civil Aviation, Malaysia

NEW JERSEY • LONDON • SINGAPORE • BEIJING • SHANGHAI • HONG KONG • TAIPEI • CHENNAI • TOKYO

Published by

World Scientific Publishing Co. Pte. Ltd.
5 Toh Tuck Link, Singapore 596224
USA office: 27 Warren Street, Suite 401-402, Hackensack, NJ 07601
UK office: 57 Shelton Street, Covent Garden, London WC2H 9HE

Library of Congress Cataloging-in-Publication Data
Names: Azharuddin Abdul Rahman, author.
Title: The last flights of Malaysian Airlines MH370 and MH17 : a firsthand-look /
   Azharuddin Abdul Rahman, Department Civil Aviation, Malaysia.
Description: Singapore ; Hackensack, NJ ; London : World Scientific, [2023]
Identifiers: LCCN 2022017926 | ISBN 9789811257209 (hardcover) |
   ISBN 9789811257995 (paperback) | ISBN 9789811257216 (ebook for institutions) |
   ISBN 9789811257223 (ebook for individuals)
Subjects: LCSH: Malaysia Airlines Flight 370 Incident, 2014. | Aircraft accidents--
   Investigation--Indian Ocean. | Malaysia Airlines Flight 17 Crash, Ukraine, 2014. |
   Aircraft accidents--Investigation--Ukraine.
Classification: LCC TL553.53.M4 A94 2023 | DDC 363.12/4909165--dc23/eng/20220705
LC record available at https://lccn.loc.gov/2022017926

British Library Cataloguing-in-Publication Data
A catalogue record for this book is available from the British Library.

Copyright © 2023 by World Scientific Publishing Co. Pte. Ltd.

All rights reserved. This book, or parts thereof, may not be reproduced in any form or by any means, electronic or mechanical, including photocopying, recording or any information storage and retrieval system now known or to be invented, without written permission from the publisher.

For photocopying of material in this volume, please pay a copying fee through the Copyright Clearance Center, Inc., 222 Rosewood Drive, Danvers, MA 01923, USA. In this case permission to photocopy is not required from the publisher.

For any available supplementary material, please visit
https://www.worldscientific.com/worldscibooks/10.1142/12872#t=suppl

Desk Editors: Jayanthi Muthuswamy/Thaheera Althaf

Typeset by Stallion Press
Email: enquiries@stallionpress.com

My appreciation to my:
 beloved wife Naimah Ayob,
 children and family, and
 members of the HLTTF & The Response Team.

Contents

Preface	xi
About the Author	xiii
Background: From Kampung Boy to Director General of DCA	**xv**
The World of Aviation: A Love at First Sight	xv
An Alumnus of Santa's School	xvii
Moving to Kuala Lumpur	xvii
MAS Interview at MARA Building, Kuala Lumpur	xx
An Offer from MAS-MARA	xxi
Training in New Zealand	xxii
Working in MAS	xxiv
Moved to DCA: A New Beginning	xxvi
PART I — MH370	**1**
Chapter 1 The Tragedy, The Disappearance, The Search	**3**
MH370 — The Beginning of the Tragedy	3
The First Day: What Actually Happened	6
How Did MH370 Disappear?	9
MH370 Made a Turn Back?	10
Establishment of MH370 HLTTF	13
Search and Rescue	14
The Good News and the Bad News	15

MH370 Ended in the Indian Ocean	17
Did It Really End in the Indian Ocean?	21

Chapter 2 The Search Effort — 25
Locating MH370	25
The Search Begins	27
From South China Sea to Straits of Malacca/ Bay of Bengal	28
North Corridor and South Corridor	29
The Search in the Southern Indian Ocean	33
The Challenges of Finding MH370	41
The Search Continues	44
Why Ocean Infinity?	46
Ocean Infinity's Search Areas	48
Preparing for a Possible Discovery	51
The Impact of the 14th General Elections	56

Chapter 3 Reality vs Conspiracy — 59
Response to Conspiracy Theories	59
Pilot Linked to Disappearance	61
MH370 Hijacked via Remote Control	61
Technical Problems on MH370?	63
MH370 in Diego Garcia?	64
The Scientist and the Mysterious Cargo	64
MH370 in Mindanao, Philippines?	65

Chapter 4 Investigating the MH370 Debris — 67
A Stirring Discovery	67
Dealing with the French Judiciary	69
Investigation of the Flaperon in France	70
Investigating the Flap in Tanzania	75
The MH370 Debris	76
Analysis of the Debris	77

Chapter 5 The Media and the Shaman — 79
Experiencing Media Scrutiny	79
The Foreign Reporter Who Followed Me	81
Stalked by a Woman	82
Facing the Media from China	83
Offers to Find MH370: Shaman and Psychic	84

Chapter 6 Next of Kins: Acceptance of the Tragedy	**87**
Declaring the Crash of MH370	87
Reaction from the Next of Kins	89
Reaction of the Next of Kins from China	91
PART II — MH17	**93**
Chapter 7 Tragedy Strikes Again	**95**
Another Tragedy	95
Retrieving the Black Boxes	98
The Difficulties of Entering the Site	101
Chapter 8 A Rather Impossible Mission	**107**
Repatriation Process of the Remains	107
Disaster Victim Identification (DVI) Process	108
Identifying the Remains	109
Bodies of Unidentified Victims	110
Managing the Bodies of Malaysian Victims	110
The Efficiency of the Malaysian Team	111
Chapter 9 An Unforgettable Experience	**115**
Handling the Bodies of the Victims of MH17	115
Reactions from Next of Kins of MH17	116
Chapter 10 The Black Boxes and Why MH17?	**119**
Analysis of the Black Boxes	119
MH17 Possibly Shot Down?	122
Why Shoot MH17?	122
Chapter 11 Forensic Investigation	**125**
MH17 Detailed Investigation	125
Responding to Accusations	127
Chapter 12 Media Reactions and Response	**129**
In Media Attention Again	129
Effect on MAS and Malaysia's Reputation	130
Chapter 13 Social Media and Conspiracy Theories	**133**
Social Media Theories	133
Dismissing Conspiracies	134

Chapter 14 The Final Investigation Reports on
MH370 and MH17   137
    A Summary of MH17 Investigation Report   137
    A Summary of MH370 Investigation Report   138

Closing   141
    Maturing Through Experience   141
    Finding Strength Through Support from Family and Friends   144
    Efforts to Transform DCA   146
    Honoured with ICAO's Highest Recognition   148

The List of Passengers   155
    MH370 Passenger List   155
    MH370 List of Pilots and Cabin Crew   162
    MH17 Passenger List   163
    MH17 List of Pilots and Cabin Crew   172

Index   173

Preface

I have always been in love with all things related to aviation since I was just a child. So when I was given the chance to enter the field of aircraft engineering after high school, it was like all my dreams suddenly came true.

I was fortunate to be one of the few who got to be involved in the kind of work that I have always loved despite the challenges and immense responsibilities. It did not matter what the task was, I would do it with much passion and determination.

I must admit, that for the eleven years that I had led the Department of Civil Aviation (DCA) as the Director-General since 2007, there had been many valuable experiences.

However, the two biggest tragedies that occurred in 2014 had the greatest impact on my life. It not only affected the families of victims but the good name of the country as well.

By now, I believe that everybody is already well informed about the heartbreaking tragedies that had garnered the attention of the global world involving the Boeing 777 aircraft MH370 and MH17.

Both tragedies had obviously great implications on me and how I look at things as a whole. Not only was I directly involved in leading the search missions of the tragic disappearance of MH370 that occurred on 8 March 2014 but I was also involved in a series of investigations concerning the downing of MH17 in eastern Ukraine on 17 July of the same year.

Both tragic events marked a new history in the aviation industry, both in Malaysia and in the international arena.

The experience of handling the two incidents was a burden that was heavy to bear and a situation that was unexpected. Let alone to a Director-General of Civil Aviation of a country facing a mysterious crisis that remained unresolved of such a scale as MH370.

It was an experience that I can only describe as "extraordinary". Even with all the training as a civil aviation officer that we had gone through and despite knowing the fact that we were required to face any kind of situation, the moment MH370 tragedy struck, nothing had prepared us for it. None of it was like what we had learnt as we faced it first hand. There were no prior cases that we could refer to as it was an unprecedented situation.

In the case of MH17, I agree with the opinion that it was an aviation disaster that could have been prevented if accurate information about the conflict in Ukraine had been obtained.

The shooting down of Malaysia Airlines flight MH17 on 17 July 2014 was a tragedy that killed all 283 passengers and 15 crew members of the Boeing aircraft 777.

MH17 was shot down using a missile by irresponsible parties that many believed could have been linked to rebels involved in a geopolitical situation.

Nevertheless, both of these two tragedies matured the aviation industry on a global scale.

Many reforms has now been done at the international level in the effort of improving civil aviation industry to ensure that the same incidents will not happen again in the future.

About the Author

Azharuddin Abdul Rahman started his career in aviation as a Trainee Aircraft Maintenance Engineer with Malaysia Airlines. He was trained by Air New Zealand in Auckland from 1976 to 1979 and continued with MAS until he obtained his licence in Aircraft Maintenance Engineering in 1981.

He became a Corporate Member (by examination) of the Chartered Institute of Logistics and Transport UK in 1991 and obtained the Master of Science in Air Transport Management from Cranfield University, UK, in 1992.

He joined the Department of Civil Aviation (DCA) in 1985 and was promoted to the post of Director-General of Civil Aviation in 2007. Throughout his career, he enforced new policies and revised directives and was instrumental in the transformation of DCA, a civil department, to Civil Aviation Authority of Malaysia (CAAM), a statutory body in 2018.

Azharuddin also represented the DCA and Malaysia in various international conferences, meetings and forums as chairman, speaker and moderator.

Azharuddin became known internationally following his handling of the high-profile cases of MH370 and MH17.

He made Malaysia proud in 2016, when he was elected as the President of the Assembly at the 39th Assembly of the International Civil Aviation Organisation held in Montreal, Canada. This Assembly is the highest aviation forum globally.

He retired from the civil service in February 2018 and was subsequently appointed as Chairman of CAAM until August 2018.

Azharuddin was an Adjunct Professor with the Azman Hashim — International Business School Aviation Management Masters' Program at University Technology Malaysia 2017–2019. He was also the Technical Advisor to Malindo Air.

Currently, he is the Chairman of Layang Layang Flying Academy, the Chairman of Strat Aero Malaysia (a drone service provider), the Adviser to the Gading Group of Companies (in the development of the future Kuantan International Airport), as well as a Board Member of the start-up low-cost carrier, MyAirlines.

Background: From Kampung Boy to Director General of DCA

The World of Aviation: A Love at First Sight

My love for aviation blossomed back when I was a child. At the time, my late father, Abdul Rahman bin Awang, was working as a chief clerk at a government office in Kuantan. We were residing in government quarters facing the Kuantan Club field, and I would often go and play football, hockey, and all sorts of sports there.

I would never forget the memories of studying at Sultan Abdullah School in Jalan Wong Ah Jang, Kuantan, from Standard 1 until Standard 5.

It was during this period that I would often see clearly the Tebuan jets of the Royal Malaysian Air Force (RMAF) sweeping the airspace of the South China Sea. Coincidentally, the government quarters that we were living in were not only facing Kuantan Club but also the Kuantan River and by extension, the South China Sea.

It was from that moment that I began to fall head over heels in love with aviation. It was like love at first sight, seeing the aircrafts traversing the sky in various fascinating aerobatics. I thought to myself how amazing it would be if one day I too could work in this field.

The moment that I dreamt of finally came true one day when RMAF Kuantan announced that they were holding an open day. My family and I immediately went there to see all the aircrafts that were exhibited at the base. It was exhilarating to be able to see up close all the pilots and their respective planes.

Clifford Primary School, Kuala Lipis, Pahang. Writer 3rd from left, middle row.

Santa Secondary School, Kuala Lipis, Pahang, writer seated extreme right.

But if there was one incident that truly opened my eyes to the nature of aviation, it would be the accident involving a Tebuan jet owned by RMAF. It crashed about 500 metres from the end of the runway.

A lot of people in Kuantan at the time went to the crash site to see what was going on, myself included. I eventually found out that the pilot was lucky to not have injured himself and was able to survive despite the crash. Furthermore, the jet that he was piloting did not suffer a lot of damage. I was able to see the damaged aircraft from a good distance.

It was then that I became more and more passionate about the subject. I would spend a lot of time drawing aeroplanes, helicopters, and related images.

This initial interest in aviation continued to develop and flourished even as I moved away from Kuantan with my family to Kuala Lipis in 1969.

An Alumnus of Santa's School

In 1969, while in Standard 6, I went to Clifford Primary School and then in Form 1, I was moved to a new school in 4th mile Jalan Kuala Lipis — Benta.

I still remember how unique the new school was because of its "newness", like the fact that it didn't even have a name at the time. Our headmaster was also famous for being very strict and would never go without his cane when he patrolled the classes. His name was Mr. Santa Singh.

Since the school didn't have a name, we decided to call it by its first headmaster ever, and thus the name "Santa School" was born. As a matter of fact, we, the pupils who studied there during the Santa Singh era, still call it by that particular name, despite it being named Sekolah Menengah Kebangsaan Setia Wangsa later on.

Most interestingly, even the alumni are called "Santarians" until today.

Even though *Cikgu* Santa was very strict, he was beloved by the students. We respected him very much. If you studied there and had never been lashed even once with his cane, then you were never really there, were you?

However, I didn't stay long. As I entered Form 2, I moved with my family yet again and this time to Kuala Lumpur (KL).

Moving to Kuala Lumpur

In 1970, my family and I moved to Gombak, Kuala Lumpur, and I immediately enrolled in Maxwell Secondary School in Jalan Sultan Ismail. The location of the site and the additional building of the school is where the Putra World Trade Centre is currently standing.

There used to be a village there, known as Kampung Maxwell. It was situated at the end of Jalan Chow Kit and thus became the perfect place for us to hang out and wander about. The headmaster, Mr. P. Nadarajah, was well known around the area for his strictness, as did the students, albeit the latter for their mischief more than anything.

On the subject of Maxwell School, the interesting thing about the school is that it was the football champion for the state of Selangor, despite having no football field of its own. The most popular alumnus of the school is Zainal Abidin Hassan, who once represented Malaysia in the football and had coached several state teams. He was a junior of mine.

While at Maxwell School, I played for the school hockey team. We would usually play at the Tamilian's Physical Cultural Association (TCPA) field which is near Hospital Kuala Lumpur (interestingly, the name TPCA stands for Tamilian's Physical Cultural Association). But since the school didn't have its own field, our annual Sports Day had to be held in Stadium Merdeka instead.

During that time, I would purchase a monthly bus pass for me to go to school. From my house in Setapak Gardens in Gombak, I would ride the Leng Sen bus to Chow Kit and then take the Sri Jaya bus before stopping at the bus stand at Jalan Ipoh opposite Bangunan PERKIM. This would be the nearest stop to Maxwell School.

But as I wanted to save some money so that I could go and watch movies at the theatres, I would instead opt to walk to school from Chow Kit. This would save me 20 to 30 cents a day.

It was usual for us to go hang out at the shopping complexes after school or after extra class or sometimes after our hockey training. There used to be only a few of them: Ampang Park, Pertama Complex, and Campbell Complex. However, the Ampang Park was the farthest, being situated in Jalan Ampang.

We would also go and watch movies at either the Federal Cinema in near Jalan Ipoh, Rex Cinema in Jalan Bandar, the Odeon at Jalan Tuanku Abdul Rahman, or the Coliseum Theatre also at Jalan Tuanku Abdul Rahman (the latter specifically for Hindi movies). If we were in the mood for a Malay movie, then Pawagam P. Ramlee was the choice.

But my group of friends were not very keen on watching movies in Pawagam P. Ramlee as it had no air conditioner. We would be sweating most of the time. We were just school boys who could only afford the cheapest tickets, which meant we had to sit at the very front in the most uncomfortable temperature. But we were entertained anyway.

Even though my family and I kept moving from town to town, my love for aviation remained as I would continue thinking and imagining a life in the aviation world. But with that came another realisation that it would be difficult for me to become a pilot as I had started wearing glasses since Form 2.

I took my Malaysia Certificate of Education (MCE) examinations in 1974. As soon as the results were out, I decided to continue my studies in Form 6.

During those days, not all schools in Kuala Lumpur had Form 6 classes available. Since I was living in Setapak Gardens in Gombak, I was sent to High School Setapak, also known as Sekolah Menengah Tinggi Setapak.

Many thought that the word "High School" was similar to the high schools in the United States. In truth, the name was derived from the fact that the original site of the school was situated in High Street, Kuala Lumpur.

When they decided to expand the school, it was moved to another location in Air Panas, Setapak. But they kept the name all the same.

It is true that a lot of schools in Kuala Lumpur used colonialist names like Maxwell, Victoria Institution, Saint John, Saint Mary, Convent, Assunta, and Methodist, and it remains that way until today.

Being students in Kuala Lumpur during that particular era was fun for all of us, since whether being Malay, Chinese, Indian, or Sikhs, we were close friends with one another. We would go out for a meal, watch movies, play sports, and do recreational activities together without racial limitations.

When I was in Lower 6, I saw an advertisement in a newspaper that Malaysia Airlines System (MAS) was recruiting new trainees for their cadet pilot programme and, in addition, aircraft maintenance engineering programme. I decided to try my luck and applied for it. I thought, who knows, maybe I could get it.

In those days, you can write an application by hand. I didn't even tell my parents that I was doing it. When I asked MAS, they told me that the trainees would be sent abroad. I was really excited when I heard it because it meant that there was a chance for me to go overseas.

MAS Interview at MARA Building, Kuala Lumpur

A month after I submitted my application, MAS contacted me for an interview. As a matter of fact, while I was applying for the programme, I did ask the MAS officer in charge if I could apply to become a pilot or a flight engineer. The officer told me that I could not do so because I wore spectacles.

I also ask MAS officers what common questions would be asked during the interview. They seemed impressed with how much interest I had in the programmes as I was asking them lots of questions. I told them that I have always been passionate about aviation.

One of the officers told me that I needed to know how an aircraft works, how it flies, what are the components (for example, the engines), and many more. Thus, I began to make all the necessary preparation for the interview in case I was called in. After school, I would go to the library to find sources for the information that I needed.

The library in my school did not have any books on aviation, so I had to visit other libraries. There were two libraries that I frequently visited in preparation for the interview, i.e. the British Council Library located near the National Mosque and the US Embassy's Lincoln Library situated in Jalan Pasar. These two libraries even allowed us to borrow the books for a number of days.

At the time, those were the only two places that had books on aviation. I don't think they even had such books in the bookstores. Even if they did, it would have been very expensive and not affordable for a school boy like me.

I found out that both the British Council and the Lincoln Library did have a lot of reference books on aviation. So I read some of them and studied a bit on the topic. I tried to get as much information as I could about aviation. I wouldn't say that I understood everything that was written, but I tried my best to digest it all for my own knowledge.

I also made time to meet up with friends who were working in MAS to get some information about the said airline. I was happy with what I got from them.

When it was time for the interview, I found out that there was a test on the topic of engineering. Fortunately, it was only on Basic Engineering. Thank God, I was able to answer the questions. The interviewer was surprised to see that I had no problem drawing an image of an aeroplane engine, explaining its functions, and several other things related to aircraft.

I remember vividly that the interview was held in Bangunan Majlis Amanah Rakyat (a Malay word meaning People's Trustee Council) (MARA), Jalan Tuanku Abdul Rahman. Why was it done there? It was because the training programme was co-sponsored by MARA.

This collaboration was known as MAS-MARA Training Programme. Trainees who were successful in the interview would be sent abroad, with their training being co-sponsored by Malaysia Airlines (MAS) and MARA.

An Offer from MAS-MARA

After the interview, I returned to my studies at Setapak High School as usual. Two weeks later, I received an envelope bearing the MAS logo. I thought to myself, have I been accepted? My heart was pounding with anticipation.

As soon as I opened the letter, it became proof that my life-long dream has finally come true. I was accepted into the MAS-MARA Training Programme. I was extremely grateful.

I remembered tearing open the envelope in front of the house gate. The letter read "You are requested to make the necessary preparation to be sent overseas. The time and location will be revealed soon…".

My father was still at work at the time, so I told my mother the good news first, that I received an offer to study abroad. My mother was grateful and happy for me. She then asked me when I would be leaving, and I told her that I didn't have the details yet. I didn't even know where I was heading.

When my father came home, he too was surprised by the news. He asked me if the offer was credible, as it did not mention when and where I would be going. Then he said that it was just a letter of offer from MAS and that I should go and meet the officers themselves to get more information about it.

I went to the MAS office to ask about the offer. The officer in charge told me that the offer was valid and asked me to wait for the updates about the trip abroad.

I also asked him whether I should quit school since I was already accepted for training programme. However, the officer seemed amused and advised me to continue my studies as usual.

During training with ANZ, Auckland, New Zealand. Writer is seated on front row, second from right.

Training in New Zealand

It turned out that there were only eight trainees in my group selected for the MAS-MARA programme. I also found out that MAS had also sent trainees for the aircraft maintenance engineering programme to attend courses in Australia, Ireland, and England.

For someone who had been selected to be a Trainee Aircraft Maintenance Engineer (TAME), I had to attend training at a school specialising in aircraft maintenance.

As a new airline, MAS signed Memorandums of Understanding (MOU) in collaboration with other airlines at that time. MAS had to establish agreements with such airlines in various fields of airline operations including the maintenance of aircraft, engines and its components. This also included aircraft maintenance training to ensure that our local trainees were trained on these specialised tasks.

Finally, in August 1975, I received an offer to undergo Training Course in Aircraft Maintenance for a period of five years. The said training was divided into two parts, i.e. three years Air New Zealand (ANZ), Auckland, and two years in MAS, Subang.

The training in ANZ was scheduled to start in January the following year (but it was started only in August). I could only go there after five months' time. That's a long time to wait. What was I going to do? Go back to school?

I had already received an offer to go to New Zealand. I thought that there was no reason for me to go back to school. I had nothing to do, so perhaps I could get a part-time job with MAS.

I went to see an officer in MAS and asked him to give me a job, any job. I could be an office boy or a clerk. The MAS officer laughed at me.

"A school boy should not be working", he said.

Soon after, I was informed of the names of the eight trainees who will be going to New Zealand, together with me, i.e. Abdul Rahman from Kedah, Zainuddin Merican and Khairuddin from Penang, Ramli from Kelantan, Zaman Khan (Joe) from Terengganu, Ridzuan from Negeri Sembilan, and Adlin from Pahang.

The time I had waited for finally came. Before the school semester was out, MAS asked me to obtain a letter to notify Setapak High School and obtain the School Leaving Certificate. Before our departure, we were provided with uniforms consisting of a pair of grey trousers, a navy blazer with gold buttons bearing the MAS logo, and a maroon tie with the MAS logo.

For the suit, we were asked to go to Maya Tailor in Medan Tuanku, Kuala Lumpur. Our pants were according to the current fashion then, i.e. the bell-bottom fashion. It was designed to become wider from the knees downward, befitting the name. Even the ties were broad.

We were told we had to look smart in the above attire on our first day.

On the day that I was to fly to Auckland, New Zealand, I was surprised to find my classmates had rented a bus so that all of them could send me off at the Subang International Airport. I was moved by their sacrifice and the spirit of their friendship.

On the first day of registration, we were required to wear our ties. We had to look smart for the pictures. However, the next day and thereafter, we put away the ties and opted for t-shirts, jeans, and overalls instead.

We were given theoretical and practical training in Air New Zealand Apprentice Training School located at the Auckland Airport for three years.

We were exposed to all the basic knowledge related to aircraft engineering and aircraft maintenance. For theoretical engineering subjects, we attended classes at the Manukau Technical Institute on weekly basis. For the practical part, we work on-job-training basis at the Air New Zealand hangar and components workshops.

The good thing about our training in New Zealand was that we were absorbed as Air New Zealand apprentices and were paid a salary. It was the most exciting part of the programme.

The money was good. We were able to live an independent life away in a foreign country. We were only 18 or 19 at the time, still a bunch of teenagers. We didn't want to stay with a host family because we wanted to be free. So my friends and I decided to rent a house.

In the first year alone, as an apprentice, we were able to give our service in the maintenance of DC10 aircraft. The training in New Zealand went on for three years from 1976 to 1978.

It was fun being a trainee in New Zealand. We were very comfortable with the amount we were paid (which included overtime). We were able to buy ourselves a car, rent a comfortable place, and even go on holidays around New Zealand, Australia, and the islands of the Pacific.

As an employee of Air New Zealand, we also benefited from getting flight tickets at staff price. In 1978, my friend Joe and I embarked on a journey to the United States, flying on Air New Zealand from Auckland to Los Angeles. In the US, our travel itinerary covered from Disneyland and the Universal Studios in Los Angeles to New York and Washington DC. While we were in Los Angeles, we even took a trip to Tijuana, the border city in Mexico.

Working in MAS

Our training in New Zealand was finally completed in early 1979 and with that all of us returned to Malaysia eager to continue our training with MAS for the next two years. We thought that we could go straight to work as soon as we arrived in Malaysia. We even informed MAS that we had been trained to maintain a DC10 aircraft. Despite all that, they told us that we were not to start on-the-job training for the time being.

The reason for this was because Malaysia had adopted the United Kingdom requirements on procedures for maintaining aircraft. What was taught to us in New Zealand differed from the Malaysian requirements. Therefore, we were ordered to train on the UK's curriculum for two years. This enabled us to familiarise ourselves with the procedures of maintaining and repairing aircraft in accordance with the British standards.

All the written and oral examinations we sat for were managed by the DCA Malaysia. During those years in the 1980s, DCA's aircraft examiners consisted of officers of the UK Civil Aviation Authority (CAA). Being typically British, all of the questions in the oral examination were detailed and thorough.

But thankfully, I passed the exams and was able to obtain my full licence in 1980. Therefore, I was able to secure the title of Licenced Aircraft Maintenance Engineer (LAME).

After obtaining my licence, I was assigned to begin my duty as LAME at the Subang International Airport. A memory that I will never forget about my first few years of working was when I had to sign a Certificate of Release for an MAS flight from Subang to Penang.

When an aircraft arrived on the assigned parking bay, it was my duty to make the necessary inspections and identify any defects or abnormalities based on a checklist.

Yes, aircraft maintenance engineers do have a checklist that we refer to when we are doing inspections. Aside from that, we also had to communicate with the Pilot-In-Command on the condition of the aircraft. If any defect was found, the pilot must note it for us to take the necessary action.

After completing all the imperative work on the aircraft, we then had to sign the Certificate of Release, i.e. to declare the aircraft's serviceability. I have to admit I was extremely nervous that first time I had to sign the Certificate of Release.

That first time I had done that particular job, I could not keep still until the plane arrived at its destination. The responsibility of aircraft maintenance engineer is immense, and the safety of a flight is crucial and cannot be compromised.

There was also a time during those early days that I had to prepare a MAS aircraft for a flight from Subang to Kota Kinabalu. One of the tasks I had to do was to supervise refuelling of the aircraft.

The amount of fuel needed for a flight must correspond with what was required by the Pilot-In-Command. Too much fuel and the aircraft won't be able to depart, too little and the aircraft would not be allowed to leave.

The calculation has to be made correctly. There is no room for error. But at the time because of time constraints during transit, I had inadvertently made that particular mistake.

The problem was that the report had stated the amount of fuel required in gallons, but I was to convert and then notify the aircraft refueller the amount in kilograms. It was because of the error in conversion calculations that the amount of fuel was found too low and we had to call back the refueller to top up to the correct amount. The flight had to be delayed as a consequence.

I had to write a Delay Report and was supposed to give a verbal explanation to the Head of the Unit, the late Mr. Abid Hasan. Who didn't know Abid Hasan at the time? That particular unit head of ours was very strict and could never compromise when it came to such a mistake.

Two days later, I was rostered to work the night shift, and it was a big relief as I thought I could escape from facing Abid Hasan. To my surprise, there he was waiting for me at his office. The minute he saw me, he called me "Young Man, can I see you in a minute" and then continued giving me a one-hour lecture on the consequences of my mistake. I really learned a lot from him.

Moved to DCA: A New Beginning

In 1985, I was offered to join the DCA as an Airworthiness Inspector. This was one of the positions created to subsequently replace the positions held by the CAA UK inspectors in the later years. The role of an Airworthiness Inspector is somewhat different from a LAME. In this job, my duties included the granting of Approvals on airworthiness related activities such as granting Certificate of Airworthiness to an aircraft and approval of an aircraft maintenance company. Other duties included conducting LAME examinations, approval for modifications to aircraft/systems, and conducting routine surveillance and audit.

My working experience as a LAME in the airlines was a valuable asset for this new job. However, to enhance our performance and know-how, we were sent to attend a specialised course called the Airworthiness Course conducted by the CAA UK at the University of Kent, UK. This training was also an International Civil Aviation Organisation (ICAO) recommended requirement.

In order to widen my knowledge in the field of air transportation, I studied and sat for the professional examinations under the UK's Chartered Institute of Transport (CIT) in 1991 and subsequently acquired the title Member of the Chartered Institute of Transport (MCIT), UK.

I also received recognition for the Best Paper Award under the subject of Airport Management in the said examination.

I then went on to study at Cranfield University, UK, in 1991 to pursue the Masters of Science in Air Transport Management.

It is interesting to note that when I started my academic year in Cranfield, it was still known as the Cranfield Institute of Technology (CIT). At the time I completed my studies, the name was changed to Cranfield University. So, we were the last group to enrol as CIT students and the first to receive our Masters' Degree as Cranfield University graduates. This university is rated as the top university in the UK for aviation and aerospace studies.

My studies at Cranfield University were on a government scholarship and I became the first officer in DCA to obtain a Masters' Degree in Air Transport Management. I was allowed to bring my whole family to the UK. It was a memorable experience for me and my loved ones.

In truth, I did plan to continue my studies to a Doctorate (Ph.D.) level and even applied to do so. The University approved my application and accepted my thesis proposal.

However, the application was rejected by the Public Service Department (JPA), so I returned to Malaysia and resumed work with the DCA.

Throughout my career in the DCA, I was appointed to several different positions which I have always considered an honour to be given such exposure which came with enormous trust and responsibilities.

From 2004 to 2006, I was appointed as the Director of Airworthiness and then as the Director of Airworthiness and Flight Operations from 2006 to 2007. In October 2007, I was appointed to lead DCA until my retirement in February 2018.

It was during my time as Director-General that two of the incidents occurred that not only affected me but also my family, my country, and the aviation world as a whole.

PART I — MH370

Chapter 1

The Tragedy, The Disappearance, The Search

MH370 — The Beginning of the Tragedy

The morning of Saturday, 8 March 2014 marked the day of my niece's wedding, which was to start with a Khatam Al-Quran ceremony (completion of reading the Holy Quran) in the morning.

The day before, my family and I had gone to the bride's house to help out with the wedding preparations and to create a more festive feel to the atmosphere. I was elected to be the head of the delegation on behalf of the bride's family and so was naturally busy with the responsibilities as well. We reached home exhausted and I decided to turn off my phone and left it to charge the whole night. I was also feeling feverish and took some medication and fell asleep.

However, the next morning, as I turned the phone on…

Zupp!

I could feel the blood gushing through my veins. There were tons of unanswered calls and messages. What was more surprising was the fact that most of these calls came from my officers working at the Air Traffic Control Centre in Subang.

Oh my God!… I could not help but whisper to myself. I had to sit down as I began to open one message after another.

The one that captured my attention the most was the message that read "MAS flight has gone missing!" and "A press conference will be held at 10 am at the Sama-Sama Hotel at the Kuala Lumpur International Airport (KLIA)", and I decided to head there immediately.

As the Director-General of DCA responsible for the supervision of civil aviation, I was trained to face anything that comes my way. But in my heart, I knew this incident would be extraordinary.

Without being able to fully understand the whole situation, I quickly showered and got myself ready to go. With just a glass of Nescafe for breakfast, I immediately drove to KLIA's Sama-Sama Hotel.

But I did ask my wife to apologise to the parents of the bride. "I'm sorry. I can't attend Amira's wedding. All of you should go on without me. Something severely bad has happened. I don't know the details, I can't say anything yet".

I had too many questions inside my mind as I drove to the location, my eyes glancing at the phone from time to time. I knew it was wrong to use the phone while driving, but I did not have any choice at that time. I was restless, both in my heart and my mind. I was plagued with so many questions and concerns. How did an aircraft disappear? What happened? What press conference?

God knows how tensed and agitated I was. Fuelling my situation further was the update that came next.

"It's MAS B777, MH370 Kuala Lumpur to Beijing with 239 onboard".

B777 is a massive plane. How can it disappear? Was it an accident? Missing? Maybe I've read it wrong!

I immediately stopped my car at the side of the road (just before the Putrajaya Toll Plaza heading towards Elite Highway) so that I could read the last message again.

Yes, it was a B777!

Dear God, ... my hands quickly went to my face. It was hard to believe. I read the same message, again and again, trying to make sure that it was indeed the B777.

There were also other messages from friends, relatives, acquaintances, and the media alike. There were too many of them, with each and every one of those messages asking the same thing: "Is it true?" "What happened?" "Please confirm the details".

Time was running out, so I was not able to reply to all the messages.

"Ah, better get the facts first".

Without another second to spare, I proceeded to drive to the Sama-Sama Hotel. As soon as I arrived at the hotel lobby, I saw my officers were already waiting for me.

"Okay, here we go". ... I thought to myself before I stepped out of the car to begin a duty that will forever change my life.

The First Press Conference.

As I was briefed about the event, they told me that the details that we had at the time were very limited.

A MAS B777 flight MH370 Kuala Lumpur to Beijing disappeared from radar screens around 1.22 am on 8 March 2014. There were 227 passengers and 12 crew members on board.

The Search and Rescue (SAR) operation was activated at 5.30 am, though no positive finding had been reported.

That was the essence of the meeting.

The Acting Minister of Transport at the time, Dato' Seri Hishamuddin Tun Hussein, was also informed of the situation. At that time, he was attending a retreat programme outside Kuala Lumpur.

At 9.30 am, we, the DCA Team, met up with the management team of MAS led by its Chief Executive Officer (CEO) Ahmad Jauhari. We discussed in brief the situation surrounding the disappearance of MH370 and thereafter MAS made a statement at the press conference confirming what had happened.

Precisely at 10 am, Ahmad Jauhari and I, accompanied by the senior officers of Malaysia Airports Holdings Berhad (MAHB) and the Ministry of Transport (MOT), stepped into the hall for our very first press conference. Everything happened so fast.

If one was to compare it to a war preparation, one could say that we were knights with sticks and leaves instead of swords and armour. But we were on the same page. "This is what we know, this is what we are going to tell".

When we entered the hall for the press conference, we were shocked to find a massive number of reporters who were flooding the venue with dozens of cameras pointing and clicking at us.

It was hard to see with the cameras flashing in our faces, and it was harder to fathom that the press conference would be aired live not only locally but also to the whole world.

Thus began the news conference for an event that shocked not only the country but the world at large, and an episode that will forever leave a mark in my life.

The First Day: What Actually Happened

Flight MH370 aircraft Boeing 777 registration 9M-MRO departed from KLIA and was heading to Beijing at 12.42 am (local time) on Saturday 8 March 2014, carrying 227 passengers and 12 crew members.

An aircraft flies through what is called an "airway", similar to what we call a "highway" on land. Flight MH370 was traversing the airway eastbound the Malay Peninsula flying over a series of abstract points in the air known as "waypoints".

A flight from KLIA to Beijing would be flying into Vietnam airspace after leaving the Malaysian airspace, and the waypoint that it will pass before entering Vietnamese airspace would be waypoint IGARI, which is located directly within the bordering airspace of these two countries.

As noted in the aviation coordination protocol, around 12.43 am, as soon as MH370 departed from KLIA, the Kuala Lumpur Air Traffic Control Center in Subang notified the Ho Chi Minh Air Traffic Control Centre that the plane had already left and would be entering Vietnamese airspace at 1.22 am.

In order to have efficient air traffic control management, airspaces around the world have been divided based on the borders of the countries or the ability of a nation to safely control the airspace with much efficacy. All of these airspaces are determined by the International Civil Aviation Organization (ICAO) and is known as the Flight Information Region (FIR).

Malaysia has two FIRs. The first one encompasses the Malay Peninsula beginning from the Andaman Sea to Johor and is known as Kuala Lumpur FIR (KL FIR). The other covers Sabah and Sarawak and is called Kota Kinabalu FIR (KK FIR).

In the years before 1974, the whole of the Malay Peninsula, Sabah, Sarawak, Singapore, and the South China Sea was under Singapore FIR. However, after Malaysia successfully acquired its own air traffic equipment and was able to manage the air traffic in its own airspace, ICAO had agreed to grant KL FIR and KK FIR to the country.

Nevertheless, the South China Sea airspace is still under the control of Singapore FIR.

In Malaysia, the Civil Aviation Authority of Malaysia (CAAM) — formerly known as DCA — is the statutory body responsible for this particular task. Each and every aircraft in KL FIR is controlled by the KL Air Traffic Control Centre (KL ATCC) located in Subang. On the other hand, Sabah's airspace is under KK FIR, with its Air Traffic Control Centre located in Kota Kinabalu, while Sarawak's airspace is handled by the Kuching Air Traffic Control Centre.

Meanwhile, the Air Traffic Unit of the airport's Air Traffic Control Tower (ATC) is only responsible for administering an aircraft to depart or to land. As soon as the aircraft leaves the runway, the ATC at the airport will transfer the control to the Air Traffic Control Centre (ATCC). In turn, when a plane is prepared to land, the control will be handed over to the airport's ATC Tower by the ATCC.

In the case of MH370, KL ATCC was monitoring the said aircraft until it was time to transfer the control to Vietnam via Ho Chi Minh ATCC.

On the morning of 8 March 2014, Flight MH370 was scheduled to enter waypoint IGARI and traverse the border of KL FIR into Ho Chi Minh FIR at an estimated time of 1.22 am. This information was transmitted by KLIA ATCC to HCM ATCC when the aircraft took off.

Thus, at 1.19 am, KL ATCC communicated to the MH370 pilot to change the radio frequency to HCM ATCC which was an instruction for the pilot to contact HCM ATCC. The pilot then responded to KL ATCC's command with, *Good night Malaysian three seven zero*.

They were the last words coming from MH370.

According to the aviation flight regulations, the pilots then should immediately change the radio frequency and make contact with HCM ATCC.

8   *The Last Flights of Malaysian Airlines MH370 and MH17*

Dy PM, the PM, Atg Minister MOT also Minister of Defence and myself in Press Conference, Day 1, 8 March 2014. Picture credit to Discovery Asia.

At about 1.39 am, HCM ATCC contacted KL ATCC and asked "Where is MH370?".

Thus began a series of communication between KL ATCC and HCM ATCC, which also included communication with MAS Operations Control room and the other aircraft that were in the airspace around waypoint IGARI. Contacts were also made to Hong Kong ATCC and Phnom Penh ATCC in an effort to locate MH370.

For the record, waypoint IGARI is also within the airspace of Singapore FIR, meaning that Singapore is responsible for supervising the air traffic of this vicinity. However, since the area was quite far from Singapore, the country had delegated it to Malaysia to coordinate the air traffic instead in that particular airspace, a decision that was allowed by the ICAO.

According to the Letter of Agreement (LOA) between Malaysia and Singapore, any SAR mission in the said area would be under the responsibility and jurisdiction of Singapore.

However, since the incident involved a Malaysian flight and we were facing a situation where nothing was certain and with a location that could not be determined, Malaysia made the decision to lead the MH370 SAR operation instead.

At 5.30 am on 8 March 2014, the Kuala Lumpur Aeronautical Rescue Coordination Centre was officially activated. Thus began the biggest and most expensive civil aviation SAR operations in history.

On a side note, we also received, out of nowhere, information that the aircraft MH370 was seen in Nanning, China. Even MAS got the same news. We immediately contacted Nanning Airport Authority. It turned out to be fake news.

When the Prime Minister arrived in the late afternoon, we had to inform him that the Nanning news was fake. We also briefed him on what had happened, what had been done, and our next course of action.

How Did MH370 Disappear?

As soon as the KL ATCC received notification at 1.39 am that MH370 did not report to HCM ATCC, contact was immediately made to MAS Operations Centre.

The response from MAS stated that MH370 was still in communication with them, with the aircraft being located in the Cambodian airspace. The information was then related to HCM ATCC. Airlines are required to have a system that enables them to detect the location of their aircraft at all times, which is called the "flight following" system.

However, about two hours later, MAS Operations Centre indicated that the information they gave to KL ATCC that the aircraft was detected in Cambodian airspace was a mistake. What they saw earlier was a Flight Trajectory projection (of where the aircraft was supposed to be) and not information in real time.

Radar recordings showed that MH370 passed IGARI around 1.22 am, and it was only at 1.39 am that HCM ATCC finally relayed to KL ATCC that they received no communication from MH370, i.e. after 17 minutes. This was not in accordance with what has been established in the LOA between Malaysia and Vietnam whereby HCM ATCC should contact KL ATCC if there is no communication from MH370 after five minutes of the aircraft crossing IGARI.

In the LOA between the two countries, HCM ATCC is responsible to set up an air traffic control service, a flight information service, and an alert system for all aircraft under HCM FIR. This includes issuing a distress message.

When KL ATCC asked HCM ATCC if they would be issuing a distress message after they have not been contacted by MH370, HCM ATCC gave no confirmation that they were taking any action.

On the other hand, HCM ATCC at one point reported that they detected MH370 in waypoint BITOD, which was the next waypoint after IGARI. However, no further response was received from HCM ATCC.

The information mix-up from MAS Operations Centre and the possible miscommunication due to language problems between KL ATCC and HCM ATCC not only wasted a lot of time but had caused a delay in the decision-making during the critical time of MH370 disappearance.

MH370 Made a Turn Back?

Since day one of its disappearance, it didn't cross my mind at all that MH370 would go missing. We thought it had crashed. If that was the case, we had to look into the radar recordings to analyse the last known location of the said plane.

We continued the search effort with reference to the radar recordings which was the practise of SAR bodies. The radar will show the location of the aircraft, how high it is flying, the speed of the flight, the type of plane, and where it is heading.

Our team also listened to the recording of the communication between the pilot and the air traffic controllers to find evidence and further information that could provide us with more clues.

However, on the second day of the search (9 March 2014), we received shocking information from the Royal Malaysian Air Force (RMAF) that Flight MH370 had made a turn back. The information was obtained from RMAF's own radar recordings.

When we were told that the aircraft made a turn back, we tried to investigate what actually happened. However, in DCA's own investigation based on the playback of the radar recordings, MH370 was noted to have disappeared from the radar screen after passing over IGARI.

The Tragedy, The Disappearance, The Search 11

With this new information, we came to the possibility that there was a likelihood that the transponder on MH370 had developed technical problems or had been turned off.

A transponder is a wireless communications device that transmits data to the radar system to indicate the location, type of aircraft, flight number, height and speed of the plane, and the direction it is heading.

If it was turned off or unserviceable, the ATCC would not be able to detect it on their screen. However, so long as there is no concrete evidence to prove that it was unserviceable or turned off, this can only remain as a theory.

On the third day, we received another shocking news that the aircraft was still operating based on an analysis that was done by downloading the Aircraft Communication and Reporting System (ACARS). The detailed ACARS analysis indicated that there was a message received from the plane that showed it was still in operation at 8.11 am on 8 March 2014.

Based on our calculations from waypoint IGARI, the aircraft's fuel was sufficient enough to continue its travel for another seven hours. However, the information received from MH370's ACARS did not indicate whether the aircraft was up in the air or on land.

Also on the third day, we were in the process of confirming whether or not the plane had turned back based on the findings on RMAF's radar recordings.

However, the question arose as to whether the aircraft in question was MH370. Based on the recordings of the aircraft that made the turn back, it did not have the flight characteristics of a Boeing B777.

The questions were put to the High-Level Technical Task Force (HLTTF) which carried out a detailed analysis on the recording of MH370's supposed turn back before the information could be announced.

Through HLTTF's analysis of the radar recordings, we came to the conclusion that Flight MH370 which had disappeared a few days prior had made a turn back.

The decision was made based on the information from Inmarsat Satellites plc, UK with the agreement of other agencies, i.e. the National Transport Safety Board United States (NTSB) and AAIB (UK). They have been in Malaysia from the second day of the incident to assist us with the MH370 investigation and search operations.

From the information gathered, we held a news conference to announce this latest and crucial discovery that we received information through RMAF's primary radar that indicated an aircraft believed to be MH370 was travelling westward after making a turn back to the Malay Peninsula before heading southwest.

Based on the earlier-said information, we decided to move the SAR operations to the areas of the Straits of Malacca and towards the Andaman Sea.

From the information received from the Inmarsat satellite data, we opined that there was a possibility the MH370's ACARS had malfunctioned before the plane traversed the airspace of the Peninsular Malaysia's east coast, followed by the malfunctioning of its transponder when it was nearing waypoint IGARI, which is the border between Malaysia and Vietnam.

The movement of the aircraft was also very consistent as if it was manned by someone who was highly skilled in aviation and then deliberately changed the direction of the aircraft.

As expected, the media began flooding us with questions to the extent that it became overwhelming and most tiring. But for the sake of duty and responsibility to convey the truth, we tried our best to cater to every question to ensure that no stone was left unturned.

We understand that an incident such as this was quite strange, especially when a plane was confirmed to have turned back but it was not known where it was located.

Based on this information, investigators and the SAR Team began making their calculations to determine how far the plane had flown after it was last detected by the primary radar.

However, our team was still unable to confirm the actual location of the aircraft.

With the new discovery derived from the information from RMAF radar, the SAR operations in the South China Sea were extended to the Straits of Malacca and the Andaman Sea. As such, the SAR phase had to be modified to involve the movement of relevant assets.

When we decided to change the location of our search areas, we focused on collaborating with assisting countries based on the evidence that was gathered, which includes shared search information and also the playback radar data recording.

For the record, the following international bodies which consisted of NTSB, Boeing, AAIB, Rolls Royce, and Inmarsat were the experts that had been with us since the first week.

Establishment of MH370 HLTTF

On the third day, Monday 10 March 2014, a special National Security Council (NSC) meeting was held to discuss MH370 issues at the Malaysian Houses of Parliament chaired by the Prime Minister of Malaysia. Since I was not a member of the NSC, a special invitation was extended to me to participate. It was attended by all the members of the NSC.

The earlier-mentioned meeting was held to discuss in detail the tragedy with the Prime Minister giving orders for all the search operations and investigation of the incident to be handled with much efficiency and transparency.

All dedicated relevant officers were directed to devote all their time to solving the crisis surrounding the disappearance of MH370. MAS was directed to assist the missing passengers' next of kin.

Therefore, a special body known as *MH370's High-Level Technical Task Force* (HLTTF) was established to coordinate the SAR operation and investigation into the case. I was appointed the Chairman of HLTTF with the members consisting of Secretaries-General of relevant ministries, the Inspector-General of Police, the Chief of Defence Forces, the Chief of Air Force, the Chief of Navy, the Secretary of NSC, and the CEO of MAS.

It was decided that a press conference would be held every day. On behalf of the government, there would be three spokespersons viz., the Acting Minister of Transport, the CEO of MAS and myself as the DG DCA.

HLTTF meetings would be held on a daily basis and a press conference would be held after each meeting.

AT the very first HLTTF meeting that was held on Monday afternoon of 10 March 2014, I felt awkward chairing the meeting whereby the members of the meeting were senior officers of higher positions than me. Although I was acquainted with all of them, that was the first time I was made a chairman with them whilst they were members of the meeting.

All technical decisions in the matter of MH370 could only be made through HLTTF, including the coordination with foreign countries, therefore the Deputy Minister of Foreign Affairs was appointed to be a member of HLTTF.

In the government's effort to investigate the disappearance of MH370, a special independent agency known as *The Malaysian ICAO Annex 13 Safety Investigation Team for MH370* was also established. At the same

With Atg Minister of Transport, Chief of Armed Forces, Chief of Air Force at the KL Aeronautical Rescue Coordination Centre. Picture Credit to Discovery Asia.

time, another agency led by the Royal Malaysia Police (RMP) was formed to investigate the incident of MH370 from a criminal standpoint.

I really had a good experience collaborating with the members of HLTTF. They gave me tremendous support even though there were times that we had disagreements and differences of opinion before a collective agreement could be achieved.

I have to admit that it was quite disappointing when I realised that there were no photographs of us, as a team that I can keep as a memory. However, we were too busy and focused on the things we had to do in the case that none of us thought about taking any photographs.

Search and Rescue

On the fourth day following confirmation that MH370 had made a turn back, the SAR operation was further intensified.

The SAR mission was not only being conducted by RMAF but assisted by the armed forces of several different countries including China, Australia, the United States, India, and many others.

Therefore, RMAF together with representatives from foreign armed forces were placed in the Search Coordination Centre to make it easier for them to communicate with one another throughout the operation.

However, the SAR could only be done during the day as it was a surface search over the sea. Related agencies would be on site from the early morning to take advantage of the daylight.

On the other hand, DCA's main responsibilities were to delegate duties, including assisting the investigation process, compiling and preparing reports, as well as handling the press conferences and several other tasks.

We were still in SAR mode during that period, as there was a probability of finding the wreckage and if the aircraft had crashed on land or into the sea, there could be a possibility of survivors.

In the early stages of the search operations, the proximity of the search involved only a small number of areas focusing on the vicinity of waypoint IGARI. However, the search location began to expand gradually according to a pre-arranged structured system. We cannot conduct the SAR operations indiscriminately and blindly because it has to cover every inch of the search areas.

After MH370 was confirmed to have turned back, the search area was widened to include the Straits of Malacca and the Andaman Sea.

There were some claims that the aircraft had landed on an island called Pulau Perak in the Straits of Malacca. However, this is illogical, as it was impossible for a plane, especially one that is as massive as a Boeing 777, to be able to land on a small and rocky island without anyone noticing it.

The Good News and the Bad News

On day five, specifically Wednesday night, I received a call from the Head of the UK's Air Accidents Investigation Branch (AAIB), which was based in Farnborough, UK.

He told me that there were good news and bad news on the whereabouts of MH370. I told him that nothing could be worse than what was happening and asked him to share it with me, no matter what it was.

The good news was that based on the preliminary analysis made by AAIB and Inmarsat which is based on the satellite raw data, there was an indication on the possible location of MH370.

The bad news was that the said analysis showed that the aircraft could have crashed somewhere between Australia and Madagascar.

However, when he stated that there was an indication of MH370's possible location, it didn't register as good news to me because the area of the said "possible location" was spread over a very large area.

Even though I doubted the information initially, we decided to accept it as there was no other choice as whatever information we could get that would help, we will accept and the HLTTF will deliberate over it.

However, I did tell him that we needed valid and solid evidence. We needed to know and see for ourselves how they did the analysis of the possible location of the aircraft. So I requested that they sent the analysts to Kuala Lumpur as soon as possible.

The team from AAIB and Inmarsat had no qualms coming but stated that they could only arrive on Friday at the earliest since it was already Wednesday in the UK.

After confirming the visit, I immediately informed the HLTTF Committee that experts from the UK had agreed to come and explain the latest analysis and that every single HLTTF member would be required to attend the crucial briefing on Friday evening.

We arranged for DCA officers to greet the UK team as soon as they landed and to take them directly to the Operations Centre at the Sama-Sama Hotel.

As soon as they arrived, the experts, one from AAIB UK and the other from Inmarsat, gave a briefing of their latest analysis and findings. They then shared the latest analysis — that MH370 could either be somewhere in the Indian Ocean or it might be located in the northern area of the Asian Continent.

According to their analysis and investigation, if the aircraft was travelling at maximum speed, it would not have gone far due to the extensive use of fuel. However considering the speed and the amount of fuel used at the time, if the plane was going northward, it could have ended somewhere in Laos. But if it was travelling at minimum speed, it could have gone as far as Tajikistan.

But if MH370 was flying at maximum speed southward, it could have been somewhere slightly to the south of Java Island in Indonesia, whilst at minimum speed, it could go as far as the southern part of the Indian Ocean.

The calculation analysis on the distance of travel of the aircraft was derived with the assistance of the Boeing Company.

The analysis done by both the AAIB and Inmarsat as above took into consideration the six "handshakes", i.e. the six communications between MH370 and the Inmarsat satellite.

Since the Inmarsat satellite is a communication satellite and not a detection satellite, the analysis made use of very complex mathematical equations and calculations. According to the Inmarsat scientists, this was the first time such methods were used to locate a missing aircraft.

MH370 Ended in the Indian Ocean

The members of the HLTTF Team and I were looking at each other following the explanation, realising that there was logic to the analysis given. We then began discussing amongst ourselves before we came to the agreement that it was the most convincing in terms of mathematical calculations in determining MH370's location at the time.

Upon reaching an agreement that the data were consistent on the aircraft communication with the Inmarsat satellites and based on the latest data analysis findings, HLTTF and AAIB have determined that the aircraft could have possibly ended between one of the two corridors.

The two corridors, in this case, are the Northern Corridor, which extends from Laos to the borders of Turkmenistan, and the Southern Corridor, which covers the areas from Indonesia to the southern Indian Ocean.

We also concurred that the analysis needed to be explained to the Acting Minister of Transport and the Prime Minister before it could be announced to the media.

Subsequently, through the Acting Minister of Transport, we were given an appointment to meet with the Prime Minister on early Saturday morning of 15 March 2014. We then departed from the Sama-Sama Hotel to the Prime Minister's residence in Bukit Tunku, Kuala Lumpur.

The meeting with the PM was attended not only by the Acting Transport Minister, the HLTTF Team, AAIB, and Inmarsat but also by NTSB and Boeing as well.

PM's declaration on 15 March 2014, strong possibility that MH370 is either in the Southern Corridor or in the Northern Corridor.

During breakfast with the PM, we briefed him about the latest findings from AAIB and Inmarsat, and the experts again explained the latest detailed analysis.

The PM then asked us for our views on the said analysis. We told him we were of the opinion that the explanation was the most reasonable and acceptable.

The NTSB was also agreeable with our opinion. The PM then agreed to announce the findings in a special press conference later that day at 3 pm in the Sama-Sama Hotel.

During the said news conference, the Prime Minister revealed to the media that experts from UK's AAIB and Inmarsat had analysed that there was a strong possibility that the aircraft was either in the Southern or Northern Corridor. The said analyses were supported by relevant facts and strong arguments.

On 24 March 2014, the AAIB Team travelled to Malaysia again to brief on their latest findings on their further analysis whereby they confirmed that MH370 had flown towards the Southern Corridor.

AAIB used mathematical analysis, which was based on the prediction that the MAS B777 aircraft had flown towards Amsterdam, the Netherlands, i.e. towards the north, whilst another prediction on the aircraft was that it had flown towards Perth, Australia, i.e. towards the south.

PM's declaration on 24 March 2014; MH370 ended its flight in the southern Indian Ocean.

PM's declaration on 24 March 2014, MH370 ended its flight in the southern Indian Ocean.

Their calculations matched with the aircraft that flew towards the south, thus confirming that MH370 had flown towards the Southern Corridor.

Based on this latest information, we briefed the Prime Minister, who was at the Parliament House at the time. He concurred with the new arguments and evidence after a detailed discussion with us and the AAIB expert. He then asked us to hold a press conference for him to announce the findings. We proposed to have it done the next day, 25 March, but he insisted on holding it that very evening.

His reason was that if we were to hold the news conference in the morning, it would have been more than 12 hours since our meeting, and there could be a possibility of the news being leaked.

He also explained that a late evening press conference in Malaysia would be a perfect time, as it would be daylight in the US and Europe. Therefore, we immediately made preparations for a 10 pm press conference for the PM to announce that Flight MH370 had ended in the Indian Ocean.

The Prime Minister's concerns about the information leaks were actually justified. As we were on our way to the press conference, I was informed that the information was already leaked.

According to the Standard Operating Procedure (SOP), any information regarding Flight MH370 needs to be conveyed to the next of kin first before we issue any official statement. At the very least, we have to inform them before a press conference to announce any important information.

However, the information about the flight ending in the southern Indian Ocean was too crucial and had to be immediately announced to the world. This was a groundbreaking news and would obviously affect the next of kin thoroughly. Therefore, we relayed the information to the MAS Team, who in turn informed the families of the victims.

I was worried that the information could have been disclosed to non-relevant parties and that there was a possibility for them notifying the media. However, there was nothing we could do if the next of kin made the decision to do so.

For the record, Flight MH370 disappeared on 8 March 2014. On 14 March 2014, the AAIB and Inmarsat informed us that their latest analysis revealed that Flight MH370 could have ended in the Northern or Southern Corridor and on 15 March 2014, the PM made the said announcement.

On 24 March 2014, the AAIB and Inmarsat further released their latest analysis that Flight MH370 had travelled towards the Southern Corridor and ended in the Indian Ocean. The Prime Minister then released the official statement on the night of 24 March 2014 at a special press conference that Flight MH370 ended its flight in the southern Indian Ocean.

As we confirmed that the aircraft ended in the southern Indian Ocean, Australia issued a diplomatic note stating that they are prepared to lead the search of MH370. Therefore, we changed the search operation mode from *Search and Rescue* to what is called *Search and Recovery.*

Did It Really End in the Indian Ocean?

People have asked me why the Government of Malaysia was so certain that the aircraft ended in the Indian Ocean.

Assisting us from the onset of the incident on the search for the location of MH370 were experts from AAIB and Inmarsat Satellite by using the satellite raw data available to them. Their analysis and calculations pointed the location of the MH370 to be in the southern part of the Indian Ocean, which they believe the aircraft had crashed into the ocean.

In the case of the MH370 incident, the experts consisted of two groups, one was focused on finding and identifying the location of the aircraft by analysing the information derived from Inmarsat's Raw Satellite Data. The other group carried out the investigation to determine what had actually happened.

The objective of the investigation was to know what had actually happened so as to prevent similar accidents from occurring in the future. It was not with the intention to apportion blame. Reference: Annex 13 — *Aircraft Accident and Incident Investigation* of the ICAO's Convention.

In general, Annex 13 stipulated that the country where the accident or serious incident occurred (*State of Occurrence*) should be responsible for the investigation into the circumstances of the accident and of the conduct of the investigation. However, due to the peculiarity of this particular incident, we had no way of knowing where it happen.

Initially, we were of the opinion that the aircraft disappeared in Vietnam airspace after passing waypoint IGARI because that was the location the aircraft dropped off from the Air Traffic Control Centre in Kuala Lumpur radar. It was only two days later that we were informed that it had turned back.

Questions arise after search analysis experts decided that the aircraft had crashed into the waters of the southern Indian Ocean. The question was: Who should be searching the aircraft and investigating the incident?

In accordance with Annex 13, in the event the location of an accident cannot be specifically determined, it is the responsibility of the *State of Registry* of the aircraft to carry out the search and investigate the incident.

Since the aircraft was registered in Malaysia, the airline was a Malaysian operator, and the flight originates from Malaysia, it was befitting of Malaysia to lead the search operations and to investigate the air crash.

However, Annex 13 also stipulates that representatives of other related countries would be invited to participate in a joint investigation. This is in view of the fact that it is an unprecedented and high-profile case whereby the aircraft simply disappeared.

The United States was also involved in the investigation where it was represented by the National Transport Safety Board (NTSB) as the State of Design for Boeing 777. The representative of Boeing Company also joined in as the technical advisor of the aircraft.

Given that the aircraft engine was made by the British company Rolls Royce, the UK's investigative body, Air Accident Investigation Branch (AAIB), was invited to participate as well.

On the other hand, China — the country whose citizens made up the majority of the passengers on board flight MH370 — was also called upon to be a part of the investigative team and was represented by the Civil Aviation Authority of China (CAAC).

Another country invited to the investigation was France. This was because France had the experience in handling investigations in the deep ocean, particularly the crash of Air France flight AF447 into the Atlantic Ocean on 1 June 2009. The country's investigative body, i.e. Bureau d'Enquêtes et d'Analyses (BEA), also participated.

Meanwhile, after expressing their interest in leading the search operations in the Indian Ocean, Australia was also included in the investigation team, it was represented by its Air Transport Safety Board (ATSB).

In addition to the aforementioned countries, Singapore and Indonesia joined the investigation as well. This is in line with the ASEAN Memorandum of Understanding (MOU) whereby in the event of a major air crash, relevant experts from ASEAN member states will be invited to assist with the investigation.

Singapore and Indonesia were also experienced in handling the investigation of Silk Air flight MI185 that crashed in Sumatra's Musi River on 19 December 1997.

For the record, there were seven countries involved in the investigation of the mystery surrounding MH370.

The Malaysian Cabinet had directed that the investigation should be conducted with much openness and transparency and that it should be represented by the aforementioned countries. Therefore, there will be no grounds to question the validity of the investigation.

Thus began the work of both the search operations team and the investigation body to locate the exact resting place of Flight MH370 that ended in the southern Indian Ocean and to unravel the mystery of why the aircraft deviated away from its intended path.

Chapter 2

The Search Effort

Locating MH370

Immediately following the incident, we started an effort to search the aircraft in various locations. Through a collaboration with Vietnam, we made an attempt to search for MH370 in Vietnamese waters as well as the South China Sea. This was the first focus point of the search operations.

I still remember that on the day of the incident, we received numerous assistance from the armed forces of neighbouring countries like Singapore, Indonesia, and Thailand. Similar assistance also arrived from China, India, the US, the UK, and Japan.

We later expanded the search proximity to the Straits of Malacca, following subsequent information that the aircraft had turned back.

The same could also be said about the Andaman Sea. Here, it was India that supplied the most assistance. And when we found out that the aircraft was last seen heading towards the Southern Corridor, Australia volunteered to lead the search operations.

However, Malaysia was not thoroughly involved in the search operations around the areas of the Northern Corridor as it was conducted on land. However, we did send diplomatic notes to all the countries in the Northern Corridor to help us find the aircraft.

This was due to the fact that it was not feasible for Malaysia to join the search, especially as it involved entering foreign territories which then became a diplomatic issue. Malaysia must abide by international protocols through diplomatic approvals from the relevant countries instead of

The countries and assets that were involved in the search for MH370.

26 Countries involved Comprising 82 aircraft and 84 Vessels

Working together: Personnel involved the air search for MH370 assemble at the Pearce RAAF base. Picture: RAAF

The personnel from the countries and the assets that were involved in the search for MH370. Picture credit to RAAF.

just entering another country's territory and telling them that we were looking for a missing aircraft.

This was especially true when utilising a military aircraft. To enter the border of a foreign country, one has to obtain a Government-to-Government's (G2G) Domestic Clearance. There are many countries in the Northern Corridor alone from Laos, Cambodia, to states like Kazakhstan and Turkmenistan.

Therefore, through these diplomatic notes, we were able to secure assistance from all the countries within the area to help us in the search. Worthy of note, all of them gave us their best cooperation in the search, even though the reports received from them indicated that there were no signs of the MH370 aircraft in their areas of jurisdiction.

The Search Begins

As many as 82 planes and 84 ships from 26 countries were mobilised in the search for MH370. It was the biggest and most expensive search operation that has been carried out in the history of world aviation.

It took around 1,169 days to scour the ocean — both on the surface and beneath the waters. The underwater search itself was expanded over 232,040 square kilometres (sq. km), not to mention the exploration of millions of sq. km expanses of the ocean surface.

The search mission of Flight MH370 began immediately on day one following KL ATCC's activation of the Rescue Coordination Center (RCC) at 5.30 am on the morning of 8 March 2014.

The search area that was announced was around waypoint IGARI in the South China Sea (SCS), i.e. the last place MH370 was seen on the secondary radar. The first ship to arrive at the search point was one dispatched by the Malaysian Maritime Enforcement Agency (MMEA).

The search mission in SCS went on for five days, with Malaysia receiving assistance from the Search and Rescue (SAR) Teams from China, Singapore, Brunei, Indonesia, the United States, Japan, Vietnam, Thailand, and the Philippines.

In addition to clues from radar recordings, we also received several reports from oil rig workers in SCS that they had seen an aircraft crashing into the waters. However, no such discovery was made. Traces of oil spill were found but were determined to have not originated from an aircraft.

The expanse of the search area in SCS was 213,000 sq. km.

FIRST PHASE SURFACE SEARCH AREAS
EAST & WEST OF PENINSULAR MALAYSIA

A. EAST (SECONDARY RADAR LAST KNOWN POSITION)

Search Area:

213,000 sq km in the Eastern SCS.

Countries Involved Search:

Malaysia, China, Singapore, Brunei, Indonesia, USA, Japan, Vietnam, Thailand, Philippines

B. WEST(PRIMARY RADAR LAST KNOWN POSITION)

Search Area :

4.56 million sq km

Straits of Malacca, Andaman Sea, Bay of Bengal, West of Sumatra

Countries Involved Search:

Malaysia, China, Myanmar, Singapore, USA, UAE, Australia, New Zealand, Indonesia, India, Thailand, Korea

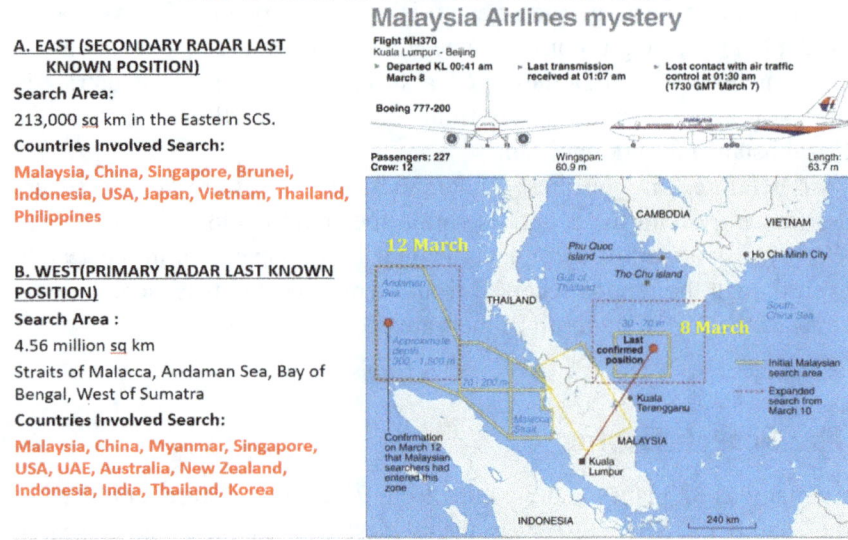

First Phase Surface Search Areas.

From South China Sea to Straits of Malacca/ Bay of Bengal

Following the confirmation from an analysis of RMAF primary radar recordings that MH370 had turned back, the search operations were officially shifted to the Straits of Malacca on 12 March 2014.

The search in this area which was extended to the Andaman Sea and subsequently to the Bay of Bengal was carried out from 12 to 15 March 2014, covering a stretch of 4.56 million sq. km. This was based on the last location of MH370, as noted in the recordings of RMAF's primary radar.

In fact, a search operation had already begun around the Straits of Malacca on the third day of the incident immediately after we received unverified reports that MH370 had made a turn back. However, as the analysis from the RMAF radar recordings was yet to be confirmed, the mission consisted of a small team. We also wanted to prevent unnecessary speculations from the media and public alike.

Our search operations in the Straits of Malacca, the Andaman Sea, and the Bay of Bengal were also joined by China, Singapore, Indonesia, the US, Thailand, Myanmar, the UAE, Australia, New Zealand, India, and the Republic of Korea.

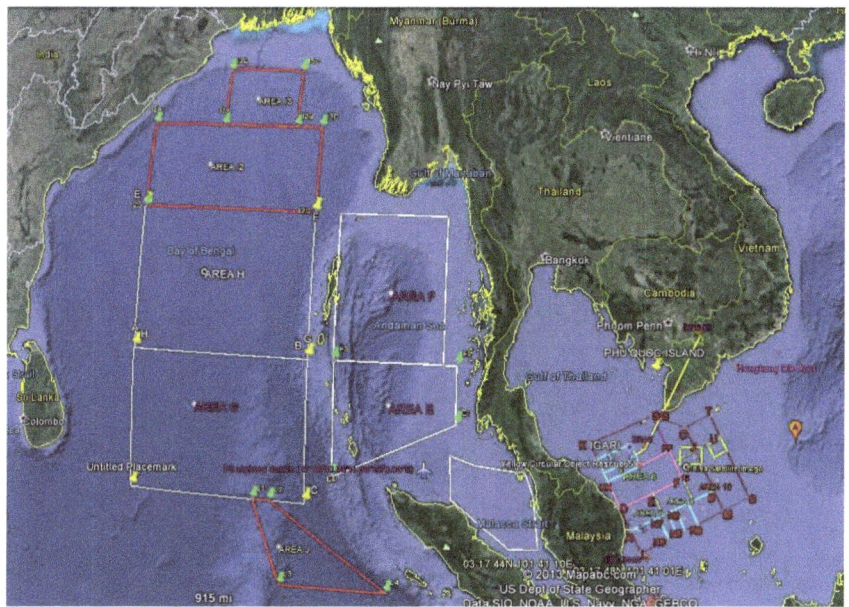

Search Areas From South China Sea to Straits of Malacca / Bay of Bengal.

North Corridor and South Corridor

Whilst the search operations were in progress, the UK's Air Accident Investigation Branch (AAIB) and Inmarsat Satellite UK conducted their own in-depth analyses of the data obtained from their satellites.

It was through the result of such analysis that MH370 was indicated to have likely flown northward or southward (Northern or Southern Corridors) from the last location detected by RMAF's primary radar recording.

While both the corridors were different from one another, the next task was extremely challenging, to say the least.

Despite being on land, the Northern Corridor stretches through 15 different countries: Laos, Thailand, Vietnam, Cambodia, Myanmar, China, Bangladesh, India, Pakistan, Nepal, Uzbekistan, Kazakhstan, Kyrgyzstan, Tajikistan, and Turkmenistan.

However, the Southern Corridor extends from the island Java, Indonesia, to the South West of Australia which consists of deep and remote oceans.

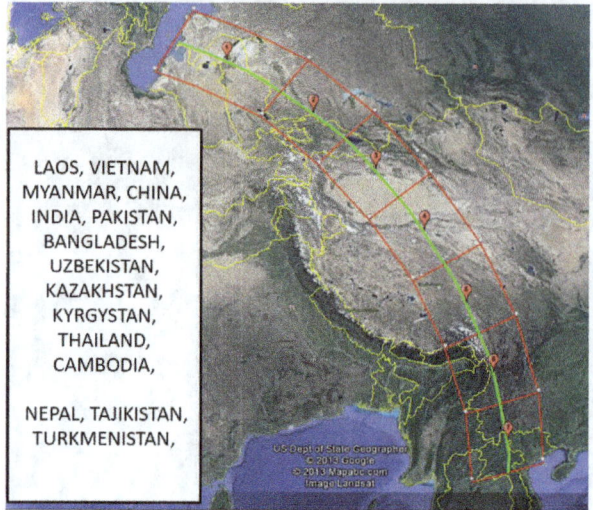

North Corridor.

As Malaysia did not have any SAR agreement with most of the states in both the corridors, the Ministry of Foreign Affairs immediately sent diplomatic notes to the earlier-mentioned countries requesting their assistance in the search and rescue mission within their own territories.

Malaysia's request became the first of its kind in the history of civil aviation at the time whereby the search for an aircraft was conducted on a large-scale operation throughout an extensive area covering the borders of multiple nations.

The request we made was granted with much positive reaction by all the aforementioned countries. However, all the corresponding reports received from these countries revealed that their radar records showed no signs of MH370 crossing their respective airspace.

No positive discovery was made through the search. Australia was the only country which reported that its satellite detected uncommon debris in the southern part of the Indian Ocean.

Nevertheless, no MH370 related debris was found following a search through the surface of the ocean via ships and aircraft.

SECOND PHASE SURFACE SEARCH AREAS
SOUTHTHERN CORRIDOR

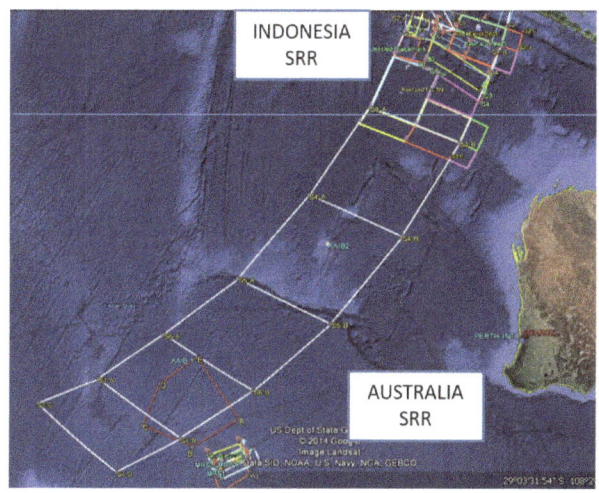

South Corridor.

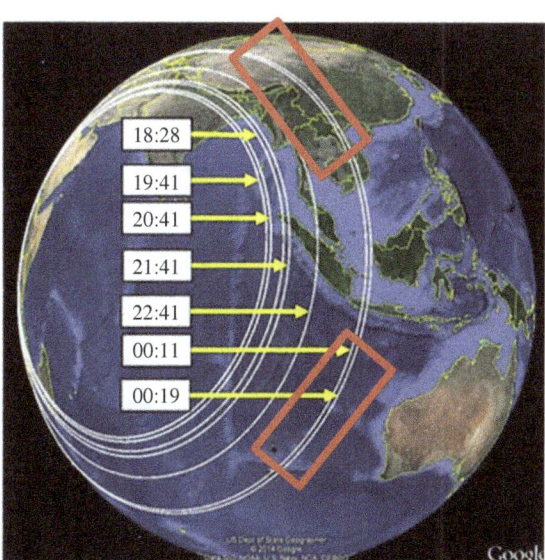

Burst Timing Frequency (BTO) Rings

North & South Corridors in relation to the BTO rings, the 7 handshakes.

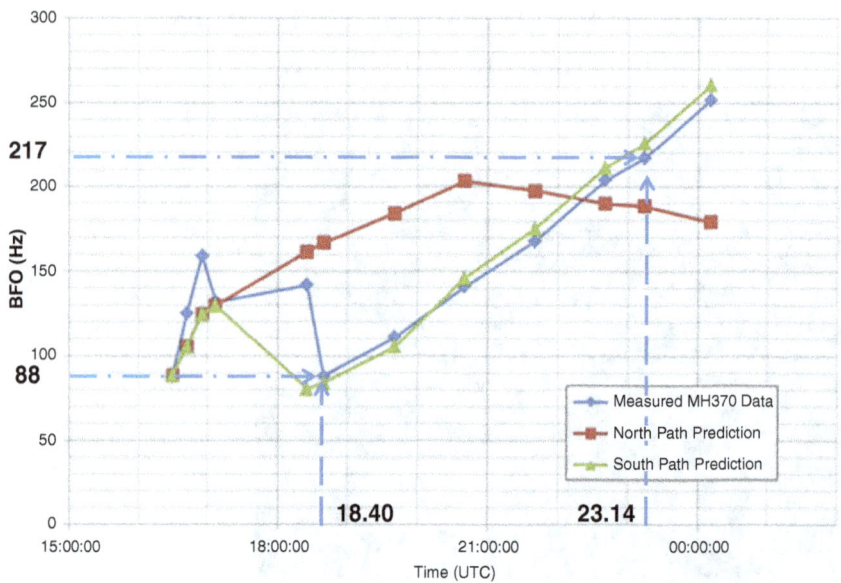

2 satellite phone calls by MAS to aircraft – BFO 88 & BFO 217

Analysis by AAIB & inmarsat of aircraft path to North or South.

MH370 SEARCH STRATEGY WORKING GROUP (SSWG)

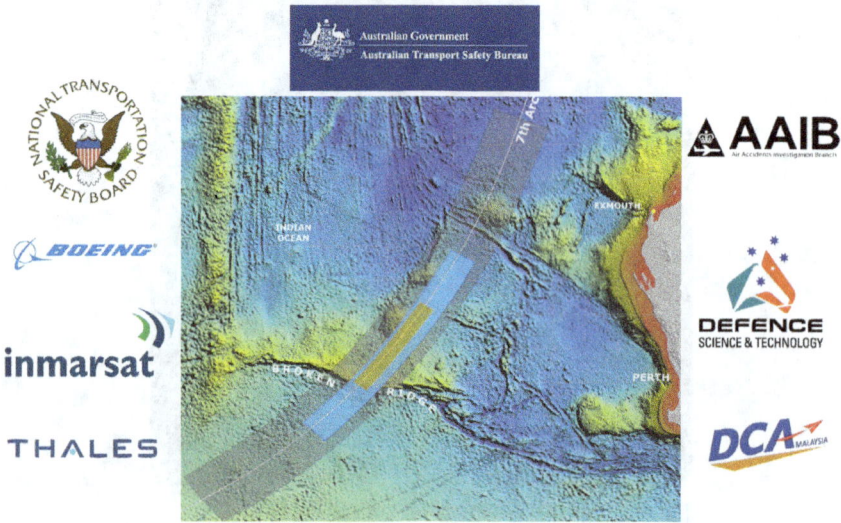

MH370 Search Strategy Working Group (SSWG).

The Search in the Southern Indian Ocean

The world was in shock yet again when the Prime Minister of Malaysia announced on 24 March 2014 that the flight of MH370 ended in the southern part of the Indian Ocean. This statement was made following the confirmation received from AAIB and Inmarsat through the analysis conducted by them.

The Government of Australia through a diplomatic note to Malaysia offered to lead the search operations in the southern Indian Ocean. This was positively welcomed by the Government of Malaysia. However, Malaysia maintains to be the authority on technical and criminal investigations.

The Australian Government established two special teams in its MH370 search operations. The first team was the Joint Agency Coordination Centre (JACC) led by Mrs. Judith Zielke, whose main duty was to be the coordinating body of the said mission. They were the ones who were in direct communication with Malaysia's HLTTF.

The second team was the MH370 Search Strategy Working Group (SSWG), which was established for the task of analysing data to determine the location of MH370. Amongst others, it utilised the raw data derived from Inmarsat satellite, as well as Boeing's performance data.

Bathymetric Phase

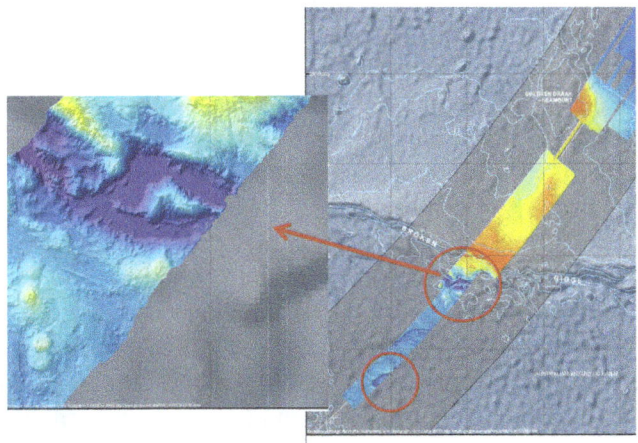

Location of search area seabed, as shown by the analysis by Bathymetric Survey.

The members of SSWG consisted of Australia Transport Safety Board (ATSB), Defence Science & Technology Australia, National Transport Safety Board (NTSB) USA, Boeing, AAIB UK, Inmarsat UK, Thales France and DCA Malaysia.

It was then that we decided that the search mission changed. What used to be "Search and Rescue" was then turned into a "Search and Recovery" operation.

The first phase of this Search and Recovery operation in the southern part of the Indian Ocean was known as the "Transition Phase" whereby SSWG located an area of search on both the surface and beneath the waters. The additional mission was to detect the signal or "ping" from MH370's black boxes.

The search operation of this phase came to no fruition. As many as 17 ships were utilised, with nine from China, two from the UK, five from Australia, and one from Malaysia.

SSWG also discovered a 60,000 sq. km area south of the transition region as the area with a high probability to be the last location of MH370's journey.

For this particular 60,000 sq. km mission, the Australian Government had offered to issue a tender to continue the search. Geo-data specialist company Fugro was selected for the mission.

Taking into account that the search area had never been explored before, seafloor mapping research, also known as *bathymetric survey*, had to be done prior to the mission.

This particular research, which was conducted from 1 June 2014 until 26 October 2014, was significant in informing the experts of the actual situation 6000 m below the sea level in order to ensure smooth operation through the deployment of the "autonomous underwater vehicle" (AUV).

Meanwhile, a Malaysian Government-funded ship also joined the search operation, which went on for four and a half months from 14 August 2014 to 31 December 2014. The said ship, Go Phoenix, was co-funded by Petronas and Deftech. On the other hand, another ship, Hai Xun 01, became China's contribution to the mission.

The contract signed between ATSB and Fugro was to last for a period of one year commencing from 6 August 2014 to 6 August 2015 with the mission expanding an entire area of 60,000 sq. km. Through the Tripartite Agreement between China, Australia, and Malaysia in April 2016, it was agreed that the search period could last more than a year due to bad weather.

Bathymetric Phase

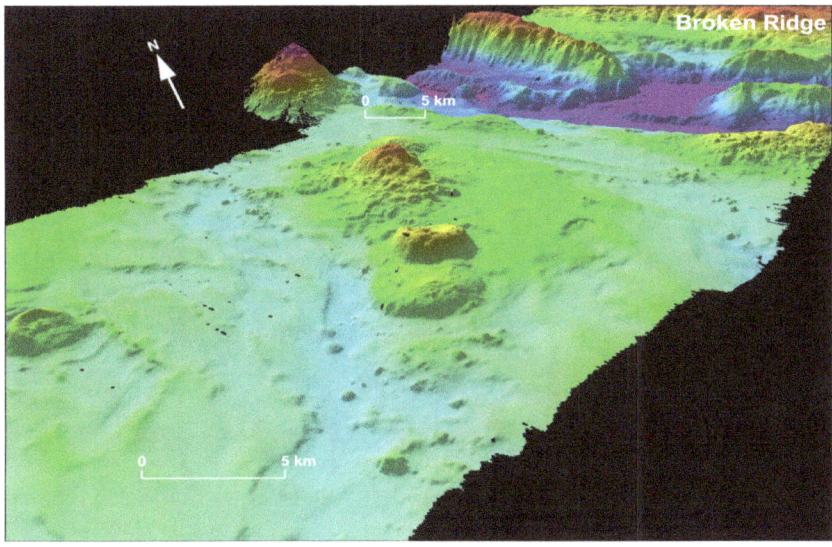

Location of search area seabed, as shown by the analysis by Bathymetric Survey.

Bathymetric Phase

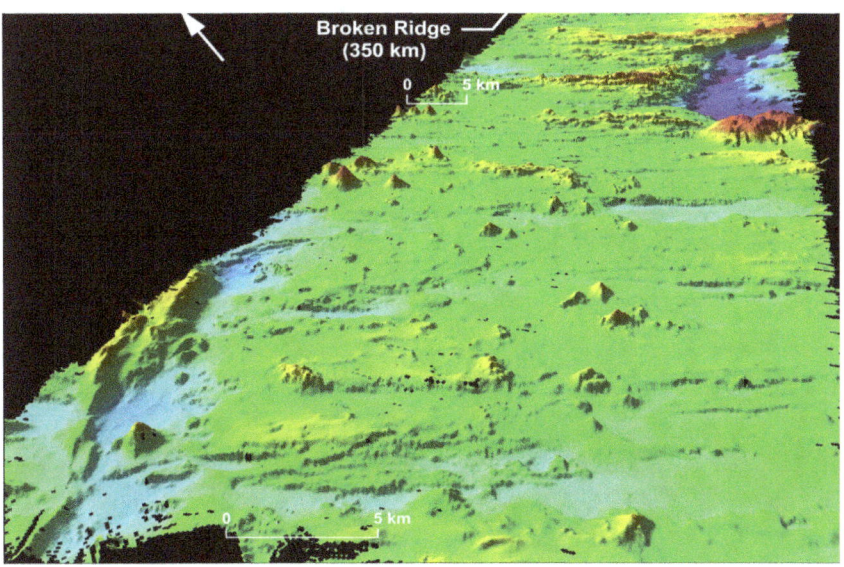

Location of search area seabed, as shown by the analysis by Bathymetric Survey.

36 *The Last Flights of Malaysian Airlines MH370 and MH17*

With the then Deputy PM Malaysia during his visit to the Fugro Operations Center in Perth Australia.

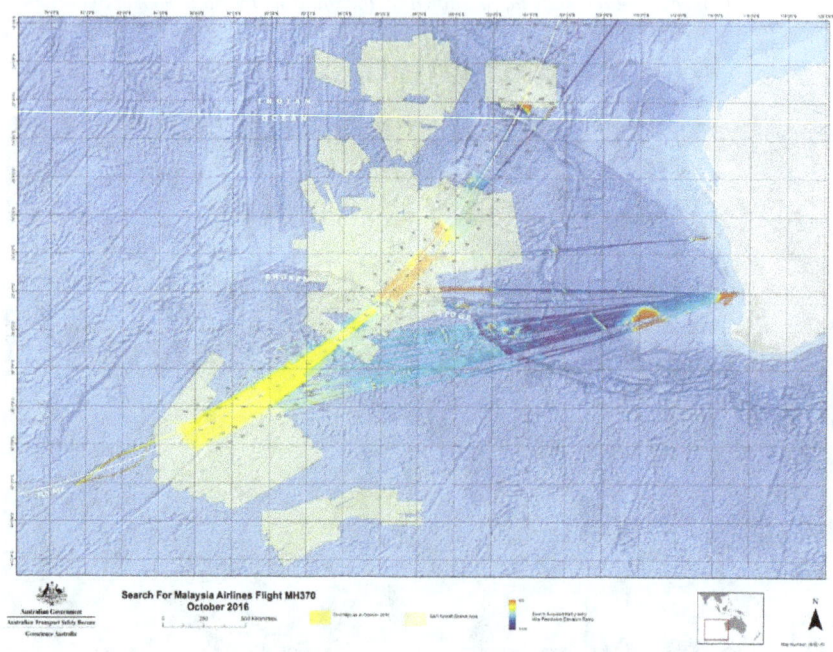

MH370 sea surface and underwater search areas.

SECOND PHASE SEARCH AREAS
SOUTHERN INDIAN OCEAN

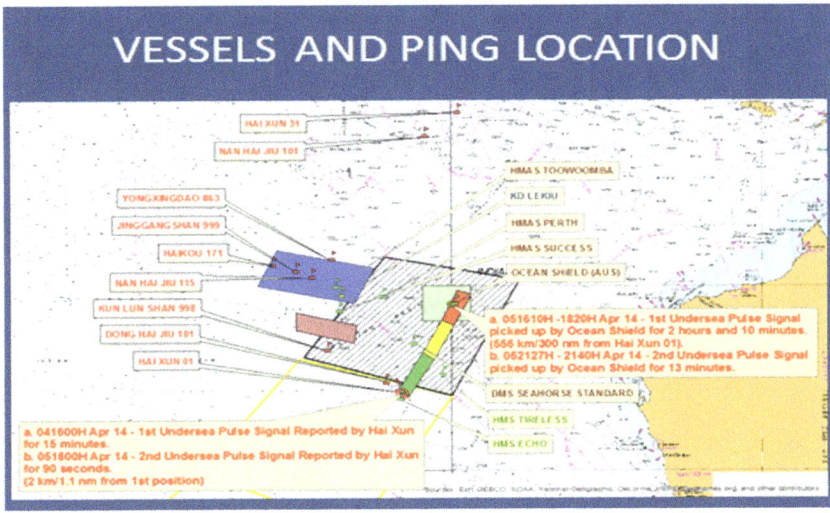

Second Phase search areas, Southern Indian Ocean.

Bathymetric Phase

Total area surveyed 160,000 km²

Underwater Search Phase, post Bathymetric Survey.

Underwater Search Phase

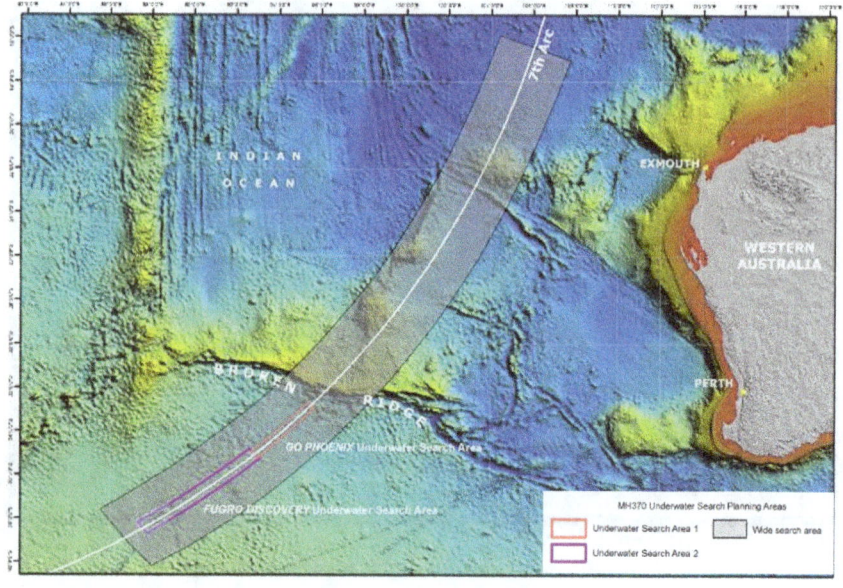

Search areas of underwater search phase.

Underwater Search Phase

One of the vessel Fugro Discovery used for the search operations.

The Search Effort 39

Underwater Search Vessels Deployment

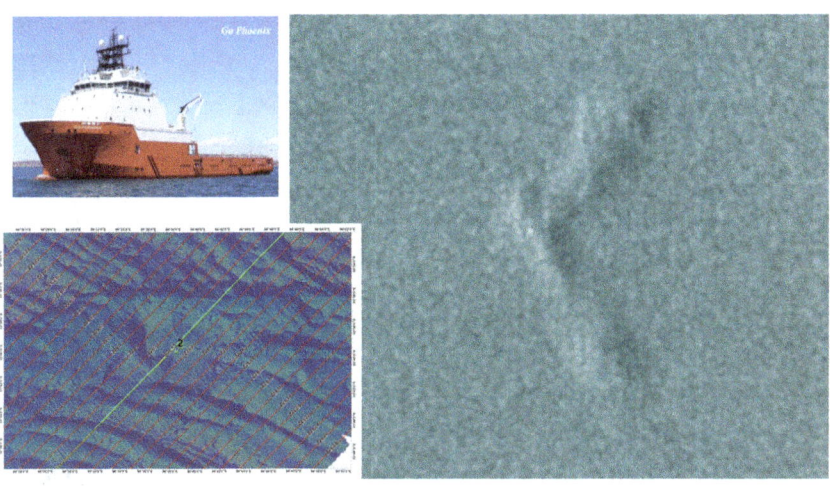

Example of sea bed image as scanned by AUV.

- ❑ Contract ATSB and Fugro Private Limited 6 Aug 2014 for 12 months. Contract end 6 Aug 2015. 42 days cycle (29 + 6 + 1 + 6).
- ❑ Commencing 1st Swing deep sea search on 18 Oct 2014.
- ❑ Maximum 120 km²/day for deep sea search.

- ❑ Contract ATSB and Fugro Private Limited 6 Aug 2014 for 12 months. Contract end 6 Aug 2015. 42 days cycle (29 + 6 + 1 + 6).
- ❑ Estimate completion bathymetric survey operation 26 Oct 2014.
- ❑ Estimate to commence 1st Swing deep sea search 12 Nov 2014.
- ❑ Maximum 120 km²/day for deep sea search.

Note: ATSB has submitted their contract with Fugro to MoF

Part of the ATSB and Fugro search operations contract.

Underwater Search Vessels Deployment

Phoenix International Search Operations Contract.

Underwater Search Vessels Command Structure

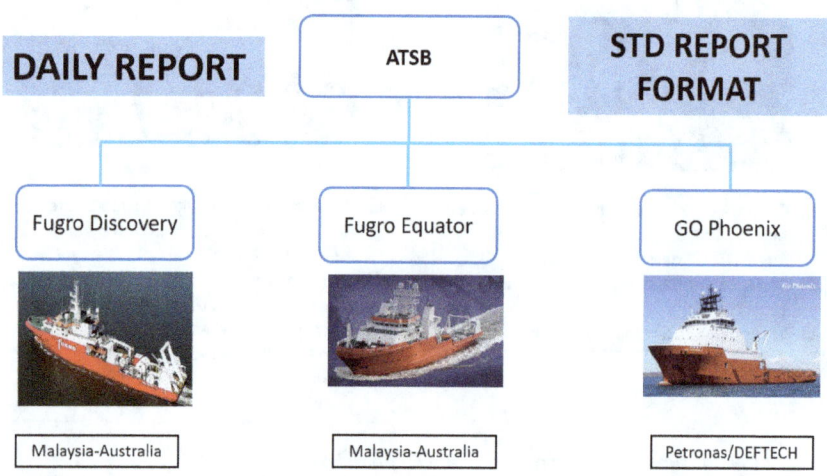

Underwater Search Vessels Command Structure.

The three nations also agreed that if no positive discovery was made in the 60,000 sq. km search area, the mission will be extended to an additional 60,000 sq. km. This would mean that the search area contracted to Fugro would result in 120,000 sq. km in total.

A meeting between Transport Ministers from China, Australia, and Malaysia on 22 July 2016 concurred that in the event that no positive discovery was made from the 120,000 sq. km mission, the search operations will be suspended until credible evidence on the location of MH370 could be presented.

On 17 January 2017, the Fugro Discovery ship eventually harboured at the Fremantle Ports, Australia. This marked the beginning of the suspension of MH370's search operations.

At the same time, Malaysia's HLTTF Team was replaced by the MH370 Response Team, which was led by me as DCA's Director-General with members consisting of the representatives from the MOT, the Ministry of Communications and Multimedia, the Ministry of Foreign Affairs, as well as the Attorney General Chambers of Malaysia.

The Response Team was established for the task of monitoring leads concerning the actual location of MH370, to coordinate with matters regarding the possible discovery of MH370 debris/wreckage, and to liaise with the victims' next of kin.

The 120,000 sq. km search operation was said to have cost a total of AUD 198 million. However, the analyses to find the location of MH370 in the Indian Ocean were still kept ongoing with reports such as the following:

(i) *MH370 — First Principle Review*, issued by ATSB on 20 December 2016;
(ii) *The Search for MH370 and Ocean Surface Drift*, issued by Commonwealth Scientific and Industrial Research Organisation (CSIRO), Australia, on 26 June 2017.

The Challenges of Finding MH370

Suffice to say, we were faced with multiple challenges in our search for the missing Flight MH370.

First of all, the location of MH370's wreckage had to be analysed by deep-water specialists using Inmarsat's satellite data despite the fact that it was a communication rather than a tracking satellite.

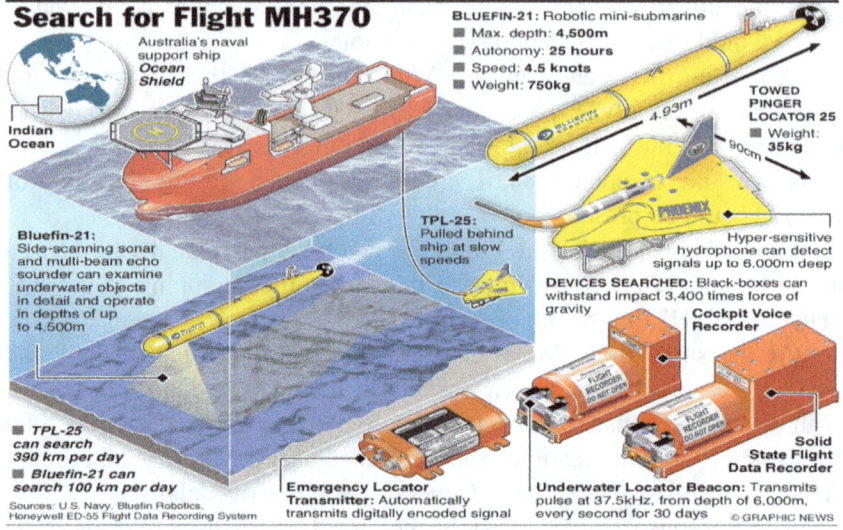

Equipment used in the search operations and the devices searched.

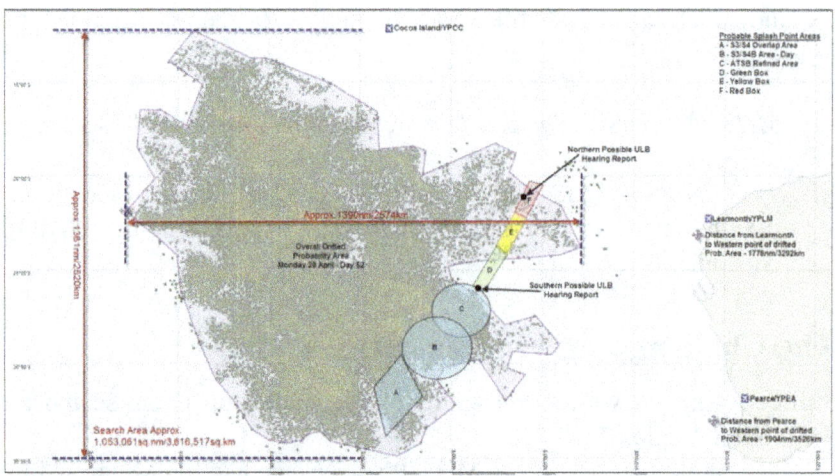

Original drifted search areas from 28 March until 29 April 2014

Drift search area.

Drift Simulation

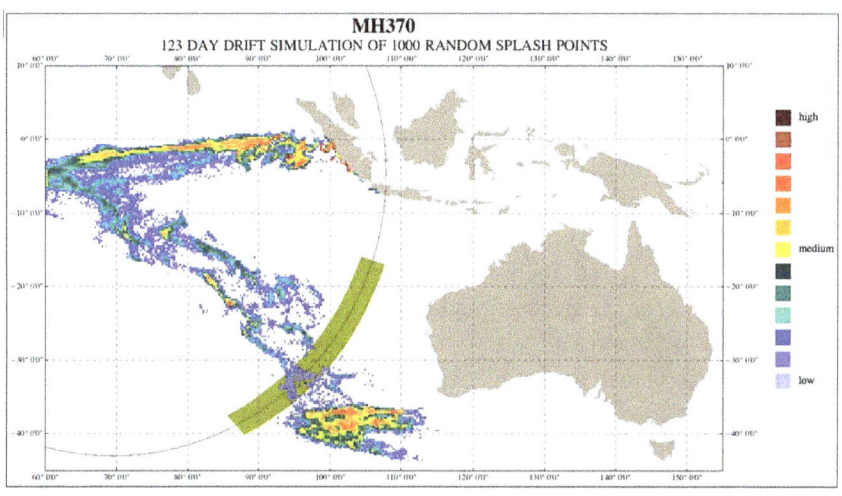

Drift simulation studies done in the Indian Ocean.

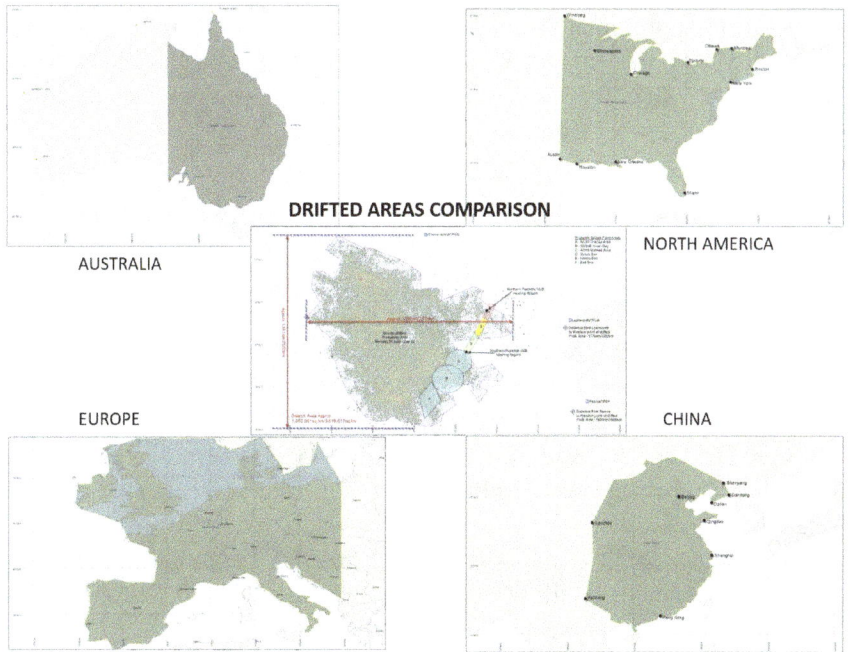

Drifted areas comparison.

Second, the search location in the Indian Ocean was extensive with a depth of 6,000 m below sea level. Moreover, the search location had never been explored by humankind and, therefore, had to be surveyed before a deep-sea search could be done.

Third, the Indian Ocean is known for its turbulent weather conditions, especially in the cold months — from its rogue waves to its dangerous currents. Such condition was unsuitable for a search mission which resulted in a limited period of operations between the end of spring, the entirety of summer, and the beginning of autumn.

It is also known that the wave currents of the Indian Ocean move very fast, pushing stronger tides extending further than normal. This posed a challenge in the search operations as there was always a possibility for the debris and wreckage from the plane to be swept away farther from the original position by the time the ships arrived following detection from a satellite or an aircraft.

Fourth, the search operations needed the most advanced equipment suited for the mission to be manned by deep-water experts. These equipment and expertise require very high expenses.

It was indicated that the mission in the Indian Ocean contracted to Fugro costs approximately AUD 198 million whereby the amount was also said to be borne three-way between Australia, China and Malaysia. It was indicated that the Government of Malaysia was said contributed almost 60% of the total cost.

The Search Continues

One can say that searching for MH370 in the Indian Ocean was *like finding a needle in the haystack*. But if you ask me, I would say *but we have to find the right haystack first*.

Following an extensive high-risk search across turbulent waters that costs an arm and a leg, the big questions were as follows:

Are the search locations analysed by the experts involved not accurate? Did we execute this three-year operation in the wrong location?

That's how challenging it was to find MH370. Despite these difficulties, the government is still adamant about finding MH370 so that we can finally have closure to this tragic episode in our history.

But with no discovery made of the wreckage, speculations and conspiracies surrounding MH370 will continue to arise.

In July 2017, the Malaysian Government received an offer to find MH370 using the services and the expertise of Ocean Infinity on the basis of *no cure no fee*.

This effort was seen at the time as one that is worth the shot, especially since the government had already forked out a huge sum of money in an effort to solve the mystery of the disappearance.

Signing Ceremony of the Agreement between Govt. of Malaysia and Ocean Infinity, 10 January 2018.

Signing Ceremony of the Agreement between Govt. of Malaysia and Ocean Infinity, 10 January 2018.

Why Ocean Infinity?

Prior to their offer, Ocean Infinity had actually made a similar proposal to the Australian Government. However, after we decided to suspend the search of MH370 on 17 January 2017, all decisions were made by the Malaysian Government.

At the same time, the MOT also announced the disbandment of the HLTTF Team which was then replaced with the MH370 Response Team.

Before we were given the mandate to sign an agreement with Ocean Infinity, we did conduct our own research into their expertise and work integrity. We dove deep into discussion before coming to the decision to seek approval from the government.

We also sought the views of experts in Australia to learn more about the company's history and background, including its technical know-how.

The offer made by Ocean Infinity was on the basis of *no cure no fee*, which meant that the government would only have to pay the company if they succeeded in discovering the wreckage.

At around the same time that Ocean Infinity made the offer, several other companies also expressed their interest in the search, including a Dutch maritime research firm, MV Fugro Equator, and a Malaysian company, TS Maritime.

After evaluating these three companies, we agreed to recommend Ocean Infinity to the government on the basis that they had the most advanced equipment and expertise in addition to the *no cure no fee* offer.

Ocean Infinity also informed us that they would be collaborating with another company, the Norwegian Swire, a maritime company well known for their deep-sea exploration and equipped with a diving submersible explorer vessel, the *Seabed Constructor*.

After we dotted all the i's and crossed all the t's of the draft agreement between the GOM and Ocean Infinity, we finally reached an agreement. We then brought the matter to the Cabinet which then approved the 90-day search operations for MH370 in the southern Indian Ocean by Ocean Infinity. The said approval was granted at the last Cabinet Meeting in 2017.

We needed to have the approval for the Agreement before the end of 2017 because the Seabed Constructor had sailed from Houston, Texas, in the US to the Port of Durban in South Africa to get it further equipped and to test all the equipment needed for the search operations.

Thereafter, on 2 January 2018, the Seabed Constructor set sail from the Port of Durban towards the search location in the southern Indian Ocean where Flight MH370 was believed to have ended its course.

The Agreement with Ocean Infinity was officially signed on 10 January 2018 in Putrajaya.

It is noteworthy to mention that Ocean Infinity had also reserved a place for representatives from Malaysia on the ship as requested by the Cabinet. We also asked for cooperation from the Ministry of Defence to position two of its Royal Malaysian Navy officers with expertise in SAR operations and experience serving on a ship for a long period of time — to join the search operations.

These officers would be staying on board the ship for a month before returning to harbour for resupplies. RMN duly dispatched two of its experts to participate in the operations: Lieutenant Azmi Rosedee and Lieutenant Abdul Halim Ahmad Nordin. Both of these officers were also equipped with portable computers and satellite mobile telephones before they were flown over to the Port of Durban in South Africa.

I initially thought that we would have difficulties communicating with the two RMN officers but was pleased to find that they could easily be reached even through WhatsApp messages and voice calls.

Ocean Infinity's Search Areas

Throughout the progress of Ocean Infinity's search operations, we continued to keep an eye on their work via our operating room on the fourth floor of DCA's headquarters in Putrajaya. The room was fully equipped with necessary facilities, including television monitors, computers, communication devices, as well as maps and diagrams of the search area and the B777 aircraft to help us to monitor the search development.

We would receive reports of the ship's whereabouts every day, as well as the extent of the search areas that it had covered. Ocean Infinity began its search on the morning of 22 January 2018 and was given 90 days to find the wreckage.

In the efforts to find the said wreckage under the deep waters, Ocean Infinity utilised eight Autonomous Underwater Vehicles (AUV) to scan the seabed. They were launched one after the other into the sea, and the images of the scan were simultaneously transmitted to the Seabed Constructor so that all the data could be processed instantly.

All of these information processes were done on the ship itself. It was handled in parallel with the scanning activity conducted by the AUV under the sea.

The ship would complete one cycle of the search operations for 26 days before returning to Fremantle Port in Perth, Australia, for resupplying and refuelling purposes.

The search areas were determined by an analysis from "The First Principles Review" report by ATSB in December 2016. Another report "The Search for MH370 and Ocean Surface Drift by CSIRO" was released in June 2017.

The CSIRO report was based on new evidence found on satellite images — a series of man-made objects that were spotted in a 5,000 sq. km area recorded by French military satellites two weeks after MH370 disappeared in March 2014.

There were four images that were taken from an area of 25,000 sq. km that could possibly be the location wherein the aircraft remained, which was a little north of the official search area.

Experts had also located an area less than 25,000 sq. km believed to have a high likelihood for the discovery of the wreckage.

In the agreement we signed with Ocean Infinity, we also determined three identified areas for the search: the first one having the expanse of 5,000 sq. km, the second 10,000 sq. km, and the third 10,000 sq. km.

Vessel

Seabed Constructor	
Design	MT 6022 MKII
Year	2014
Length	115.4m
Breadth	22m
Accommodation	102 PAX
Crane	250 Tonne AHC
Moonpool	7.2m x 7.2m
Cargo Deck	1300 m²

Vessel used by Ocean Infinity, the Seabed Constructor.

Equipment

The equipment used in the Ocean Infinity search operations.

OI Equipment in Operation

Ocean Infinity in operations.

In the event that no discovery was made in the aforementioned areas, Ocean Infinity would then conduct a search outside the agreed areas, which would be the locations recommended by experts based on investigation reports released by ATSB. This would mean that the search areas would no longer be determined by the government but by the experts looking for MH370.

On 8 February 2018, I was tasked to travel to the Fremantle Port to see for myself the progress of the search made by Ocean Infinity. I also had the opportunity to meet with our representatives on board the Seabed Constructor.

The ship set sail again towards the search location on 13 February 2018 and began exploring the primary area within the expanse of 7,000 sq. km.

Ocean Infinity was able to conduct a rapid search as they were using up to eight AUVs simultaneously and was able to operate at a depth of between 5,000 and 6,000 metres.

These AUVs were capable of handling the mission freely in order to gather high-quality data. In just one day, it could cover a length of 1,000 km.

For every week on Tuesdays, we would submit weekly reports about the search operation to the next of kin before subsequently releasing it to the media.

We did pay much attention to the sensitivity of the victim's family members. Thus, for the victim's family in China, we would send the reports to MAS to be translated to Mandarin before delivering them to the next of kins through our website.

At the same time, we also submitted reports to the MOT of Malaysia as well as the Australian and Chinese Governments. It was only after that we were finally able to release the weekly reports on DCA's official website for the media and public knowledge.

Preparing for a Possible Discovery

We actually had already arranged preparatory work in the event that a discovery is made of MH370. In this scenario, Ocean Infinity will inform us of the discovery through DCA's operation centre. The Response Team will immediately meet and discuss with experts consisting of investigators and the team from MAS, in particular, those who have worked on a B777 aircraft, to confirm whether or not the discovered wreckage is indeed MH370.

For confirmation, the Ocean Infinity Team will have to forward images that will clearly indicate the wreckage and related debris of MH370.

Next, we will request for additional timeframe if there is any need for more information. If the wreckage found is confirmed to be MH370, we will then inform the Minister of Transport and he, in turn, will contact the Prime Minister to officially announce the discovery.

In the event that the wreckage is officially found, we also have our own SOP on what needs to be done. It is imperative that we take immediate and correct action so such a situation may not be exploited, edited and made viral as fake news.

It is also important to remember that any new announcement about MH370 needs to be relayed to the next of kin first and foremost. There were many out there who had been following the progress of the search operation.

We will also have to discuss the search and recovery phase and what we are required to do to establish a thorough recovery plan.

52 *The Last Flights of Malaysian Airlines MH370 and MH17*

Ocean Infinity search areas.

SEARCH AREAS BASED ON

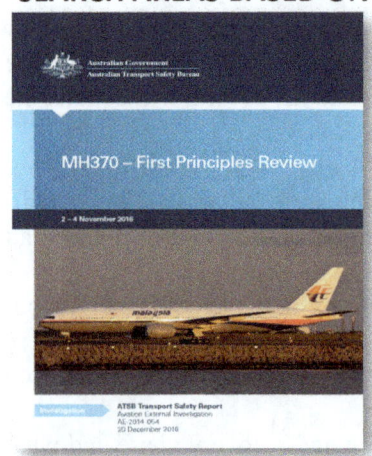

- Released on 20 December 2016 by Australian Transport Safety Board (ATSB)
- Discussed on an area of search of 25,000 km² between 32.5º south and 36.0º south along the 7th arc

The Report that was used for the Ocean Infinity search operations.

The Search Effort 53

SEARCH AREA

Purple shading represents the
TERTIARY SEARCH AREA 3 **which is** 10,000 km²

Green shading represents the
SECONDARY SEARCH AREA **which is**
10,000 km²

Orange shading represents the
PRIMARY SEARCH AREA **which is**
5,000 km²

Ocean Infinity search areas.

SEARCH AREAS BASED ON

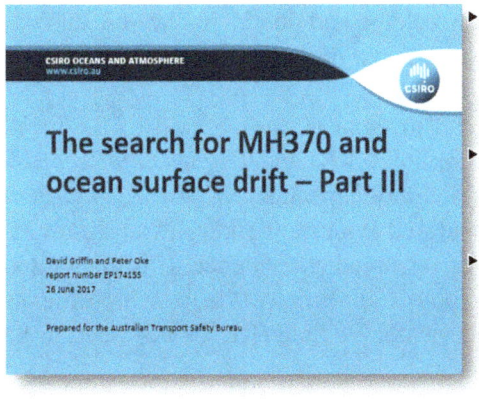

- The report issued by the CSIRO and ATSB on 26 June 2017 report identified a number of objects in the satellite imagery acquired
- These findings had narrowed down the earlier analysis from the First Principle Review Report
- Focused to an area of 5,000 km² of the 25,000 km² as the most likely location of the aircraft.

The Report that was used for the Ocean Infinity search operations.

Through this plan, if a discovery has been made, we will send a team of investigators on board the Seabed Constructor to ensure only crucial debris are recovered for investigation.

The investigation itself will consist of two different areas: one technical and the other criminal. Therefore, investigation experts of both areas have to be at the location where MH370 is found. Ocean Infinity's mission is to find the wreckage of the aircraft and confirm it according to the procedure that has been determined in the agreement with the Malaysian Government and not for investigative purposes.

We were well aware that we had only given Ocean Infinity a search period of 90 days. However, there was a clause in the agreement stipulating that the search operations can be continued if warranted subject to the situation at the time whereby the decision would depend solely on the Government. If Ocean Infinity was to request for a continuation of the search operations, we will then proceed with a negotiation with them before we submit for approval from the Government. Ocean Infinity will provide reasons for the continuation and areas of search operations if it is outside the area of search as in the Agreement.

Ocean Infinity seemed very confident. If the wreckage can be found in the 90 days' time as in the Agreement, they will have no qualms retrieving any evidence that we require.

We understand that retrieving evidence would not be easy and would be very costly. We were already briefed about it by the experts who were involved in the search of Air France AF447 that crashed into the Atlantic Ocean in 2009.

In the event of a discovery, Ocean Infinity has to create a map of the surrounding area to indicate the wreckage and debris discovered, such as engines, wings or related objects. The area of the map is called the *debris field*.

Another priority of the second mission is the retrieval of the black boxes, i.e. the *Cockpit Voice Recorder* (CVR) and *Flight Data Recorder* (FDR), in order to find out what actually happened.

Anything that could be considered important and relevant to investigation experts would have to be retrieved as evidence. It is also noted that the depth of the ocean is about 6,000 metres deep, which means that the unmanned Remote Underwater Vehicle (RUV) will need to be used.

The RUV will be lowered into the deep seabed to retrieve and bring to surface materials related directly onto the ship. This is because at

Visit to the Ocean Infinity AUV storage area in the Seabed Constructor vessel, 8 February 2018.

Visit to the Ocean Infinity AUV storage area in the Seabed Constructor vessel, 8 February 2018.

Visit to the Seabed Constructor, Ocean Infinity Operations Center, 8 February 2018.

6,000 metres below sea level, the intensity of the air pressure is very high, which would be impossible for any human being to survive.

The Impact of the 14th General Elections

I would like to share with you an experience of mine whereby during the course of the search operations, I was plagued with a dilemma that left me with many a sleepless night.

As I have shared earlier, Ocean Infinity had offered to conduct the operation through *no cure no fee* basis, with payment to be made to them if they were able to find the wreckage of the aircraft within 90 days.

However, on April 2018, once Ocean Infinity's contract expired, they made a request for it to be extended until the end of May. The Government at the time decided to approve the request for an extension of the contract but only until 6 May 2018.

When it expired for the second time, Ocean Infinity again made another request for an extension.

The problem was, at the time, Malaysia was experiencing a historic event that was the 14th General Election which was on 9 May 2018. We all know what happened. The then incumbent the *Barisan Nasional* (National Front) was defeated by *Pakatan Harapan*, resulting in a change of government.

During the period when the Ocean Infinity Team was requesting another extension, the Cabinet was yet to be fully formed. The team was even willing to travel all the way to Putrajaya in order to set a meeting with the MOT. The problem was that the new Minister of Transport had yet to be appointed then.

Following the forming of the new Cabinet, my main duty was to meet with the new Transport Minister to request an extension of Ocean Infinity's contract. The newly formed Malaysian Government agreed to do so but only until 29 May 2018. Further than that, there would be no more necessity for them to search for the aircraft.

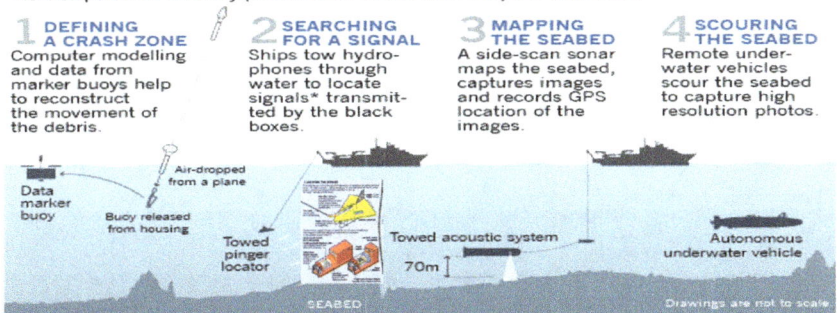

Search and Recovery phases, whenever MH370 wreckage found.

As for Ocean Infinity, the search operation was conducted based on the two previously mentioned reports. However, with no discovery made in the determined locations, they had extended the search areas further.

Therefore, throughout the period before 6 May 2018, I was turning on my phone every day and praying for the discovery of MH370 wreckage.

After the said date, despite the fact that they were yet to get the approval from the government to extend their contract, the Ocean Infinity Team decided to continue with the search, even though we have not received approval from the Government.

I asked them "You know what will be the consequences?".

What I meant was, if they were to find MH370 during that period, the biggest concern would be they might not get paid, since the government had not yet agreed to an extension of the contract after 6 May.

They replied "Don't worry. We know what to do".

Thus, after the contract expired, with an extension yet to be agreed upon, I spent a lot of my time checking on my phone anxiously.

If Ocean Infinity succeeded in finding the aircraft within the search areas, they were entitled to a payment of up to USD 70 million. That is such a hefty amount. The problem was that we had yet to get the approval from the government to continue with the mission. If that was the case, who will be paying them?

Considering the above, I was extremely concerned that we would not be able to make the payment if MH370 were to be found, however at the same time, deep inside, I was hoping that the wreckage of MH370 would be finally be found so that the mystery will be finally be solved.

Chapter 3

Reality vs Conspiracy

Response to Conspiracy Theories

To this day, there have been lots of theories being thrown out there by various parties around the world, be it from an authority or from those who believed in such conspiracy theories surrounding the disappearance of MH370. But if you ask me, those theories are just that, theories.

People can say what they want and share whatever opinion they have, especially the ones that only trigger more speculations. We still hear a lot of stories and reports about the disappearance though most of the evidence given is questionable at best.

The fact of the matter is this: there were seven countries involved in the investigation surrounding the disappearance of MH370. The process adhered to the procedures presented by Annex 13 of the ICAO Convention. It was a high-profile accident involving international investigation which meant that the work done was thorough and based on actual facts.

Furthermore, China was also very scrupulous with regards to the investigation that we conducted and demanded it to be wholly transparent and thorough. The Public Security Bureau of China would also show up from time to time to learn more about the progress of the search.

In many cases, we need to share the information that we got from the investigation. No matter how little we found, we still informed others about it.

China had also dispatched its military to participate in the search mission for MH370. While the unfortunate aircraft belonged to us, the operation involving deep-sea search was led by Australia. All the three countries agreed that there should be a Tripartite Agreement not only in conducting the search efforts but also in handling the next of kin.

According to the said agreement, if one of the countries was showing opposition against a decision, this would pose a big problem since the effort involved the collaboration of all three. I was thankful that there had been no issue throughout the cooperation despite our many differences of opinion. This was due to the fact that the Transport Ministers of all three countries demonstrated a high spirit of camaraderie when it came to finding solutions for the next of kin.

It was admittedly challenging at first, especially as it involved communicating in different languages that could easily be misinterpreted. The Chinese Government's biggest priority was its citizens who were involved in the tragedy of MH370.

They would always inform the family of the victims of any news and ensured that all related information must first be relayed to the next of kin. We understood how sensitive they were and still are about the tragedy. Until today, some of them are still unwilling to accept that the aircraft is gone.

The conspiracy theories concerning what had happened to MH370 without substantial evidence had attracted the world's attention. It had sparked a lot of interesting theories about what actually happened leading to countless debates and discussions about the tragedy to this very day.

According to the international air traffic management standard practices, aircraft around the world travel across the sky using air routes which are called airways through abstract points which are known as waypoints. This means that an aircraft would be flying through the airways and traversing from one waypoint to the other.

When we analysed the radar recordings of Flight MH370 after it made a turn back, we found that it was traversing from one waypoint to another before disappearing from radar coverage.

In view of the above, some aviation experts had come to the opinion that the plane was manned by a "pilot" who knew what he or she was doing.

That led to the most popular question, who was actually flying the aircraft.

Pilot Linked to Disappearance

Many aviation experts opined that there was the possibility that the decision to turn MH370 around was made by a pilot. This was considered logical since only an experienced pilot would be able to do such a maneuver.

In this particular case, if it is true that a pilot had decided to do this, where was the co-pilot who was with him? This theory is questionable, as there would be no reason for a pilot and his co-pilot to conspire in turning the plane around unless they were faced with technical problems during the flight.

It does not make sense for both the pilot and the co-pilot to risk the lives of hundreds of passengers as well as their colleagues.

There was also a claim that the pilot had been forced to turn the plane around probably by someone inside the cockpit who demanded that they flew the plane to the last of its fuel until it crashed into the ocean. This was a possibility too. However, there was no solid evidence to support this claim.

Another theory alleged that MH370 was flown to a height of 40,000 ft by a pilot who was equipped with an oxygen mask and with the intention to suffocate the passengers and cabin crew due to hypoxia, i.e. lack of oxygen, therefore giving the pilot the freedom to fly the aircraft until it crashed. Some aviation experts are of the view that whether it be autopilot or manual, an aircraft could not fly to that height without proper training and experience.

So, here we can say that these are all theories. We do not have the evidence to say it was the MH370 pilot or the co-pilot or a third party who made the decision to turn the aircraft back. This remains a mystery to all of us.

That was also the reason why Australia, China and Malaysia gave their best effort and invested a lot of resources into finding the MH370 wreckage, especially the black boxes. Only by uncovering the information from the black boxes we can finally discover what had actually happened during the flight.

MH370 Hijacked via Remote Control

The second most prominent theory was that the pilot himself flew the plane but was doing so under the coercion of another, meaning that the plane was hijacked. However, we do not have solid evidence to back this theory for now.

Whatever has being rumoured and viraled out there is still just a theory. We cannot confirm any of it because none were supported by solid evidence. Moreover, in the case of hijacking, there is always a specific group involved and they would almost certainly admit to the crime immediately after such incident.

Until now no individual or group has stepped forward to confess to such claims. This could be because there was no motive for such action.

Another theory stated that MH370 might have been controlled by a different aircraft through a remote device. There is a logical side to this argument. It cannot be denied that there is a technology that can do just that. However, that particular aircraft must be equipped with the most advanced technologies.

In my personal opinion, it would be impossible for MH370 to be controlled from afar. It was not feasible for a remote control device to be installed on the said aircraft during the incident.

For one to equip such a device on a plane, one would need at least two weeks to install the electronics and handle all the wiring on the plane itself. Prior to its departure from KLIA to Beijing in the wee morning of 8 March 2014, MH370 was parked in KLIA for eight hours following its prior journey. Thus, it would be impossible for someone to install all the electronic devices in such a short time.

There are also speculations that a passenger on board the flight was involved in the hijacking or that there were people who were controlling the plane remotely from a different aircraft.

From a technical side, a person who plans to control a plane as massive as MH370 remotely needs to have a detailed plan and elaborate work done. The perpetrator would also need a communication device like a satellite or other available equipment.

Hijacking a plane using a remote control is not as easy as it sounds. For this plan to work, the plane would need to be equipped with the aforementioned equipment and tools. These are not your ordinary electronics, and one will need expertise in installing them.

Such installation would also take a long time, whereas MH370 was only in KLIA for eight hours after it arrived from its previous destination. This meant that one would have only eight hours to install all the necessary devices prior to hijacking the aircraft. This is such an impossible situation.

On the other hand, Boeing has also released a statement saying that it would be impossible for MH370 to be hijacked remotely since such technology has never been applied to any commercial aircraft.

Technical Problems on MH370?

There was another speculation that had arisen about the flight which was that a fire had occurred and smoke was coming from the cabin. However, in the event of a fire, it would have been impossible for the aircraft to fly for another eight hours. Furthermore, the pilot would have contacted and alerted the ATC of the situation.

Even if there was a technical problem and the pilot was forced to fly the plane, the pilot could still notify the ATC by simply pressing a switch which was easily accessible to the pilot in the cockpit when trouble arises. This will directly notify the nearby ATC that the aircraft is experiencing problems or interruptions.

The question is: Why was there no response at all from the pilot when the plane was contacted by the ATC? It is noted that we also had requested for nearby aircraft to make contact with MH370 shortly following its disappearance. However, no response had been received from the said aircraft.

Therefore, only the information from the black boxes could give an insight into what had actually happened to the aircraft.

The black boxes consist of two different equipment. One is called the Cockpit Voice Recorder (CVR) while the other the Flight Data Recorder (FDR).

A CVR will digitally record the last two hours of audio communications between pilots, their interaction with ATC, and any other sounds inside the cockpit. The last two hours means that the recordings would consist of audio signals of the plane in its flying phase, its landing phase, or in some cases, during the crash.

There is a likelihood that no important evidence was even recorded in the last two hours of MH370's CVR. The most critical phase for an investigation is the period before and after the plane had made the turn back. Unfortunately, since the time lapse from the turn back and the crash exceeded more than 2 hours, that part of the CVR recordings would have been automatically deleted by the device.

In view of the above, we would need to rely only on the FDR recordings to obtain the critical information. The FDR is capable of recording more than 100 parameters, which records the condition of a plane, its equipment, and components in the last 25 hours of flight.

Thus, the theories about the plane being on fire or having technical problems remain as theories.

MH370 in Diego Garcia?

A lot of people seemed to believe that MH370 had been flown to the island of Diego Garcia. But, again, we need solid evidence and confirmed facts without which is just another theory.

Diego Garcia is a US militarised atoll situated in the northern part of the Indian Ocean. It actually belongs to the United Kingdom but was leased to the United States. Logically, nobody could approach the area without permission.

Therefore, in the case, we had to obtain the information from the US Embassy in Kuala Lumpur. They had released a statement stating that the aircraft had never landed on Diego Garcia.

The Scientist and the Mysterious Cargo

There were others who expressed doubt and concern regarding several cargoes that were on Flight MH370. Among the cargo in question was one containing a large number of mangosteens. Some wondered why there were so many mangosteens inside the aircraft when it was not in season in Malaysia.

When we checked on that, we found out that it was not the first time that mangosteens had been sent using MASkargo consignment using MAS passenger aircraft. What's more, it was not Malaysian mangosteens but was delivered from a neighbouring country.

There were also questions on the cargo containing lithium batteries that were on board the aircraft. Yes, there were concerns about batteries starting a fire, but it is not unusual for lithium batteries to be delivered via aircraft, not to mention that smartphones have lithium batteries as well.

While investigating the case earlier on, we found out that the lithium batteries in question were made in Penang and had been packed according to its required packaging standards.

There were also concerns that the mangosteens emit a type of inflammable gas which could have come into contact with the lithium batteries causing a fire. Tests were carried out by the investigators which found that such claims were not true. Refer Safety Investigation Report, Section 2.8, Aircraft Cargo Consignment.

Some even suggested that there was a scientist who was carrying uranium on board the plane. If that was the case, that particular passenger would have been detained by the security personnel following an X-ray scan before he or she could even board the aircraft.

The authority concerned had also profiled each and every passenger and found no one that could meet the description of that particular scientist. They even profiled the crew members working aboard the aircraft that day and it was concluded that nothing suspicious had been found.

MH370 in Mindanao, Philippines?

I would also like to share a story that had gone viral at the end of 2016 whereby an unknown person had claimed to have found the wreckage of an aircraft in "red and blue" on the Philippine island of Mindanao.

Before we decided on whether or not to believe the aforementioned information which was received through an email, we approached the Ministry of Foreign Affairs for advice. We were then asked to refer to the RMP's Intelligence Unit.

The RMP Intelligence Team subsequently advised us not to over trust the information because the location where the wreckage was supposedly found was in an area controlled by Moro rebels.

Based on the advise of RMP, we responded to the email and asked them to inform us of the exact location where the wreckage was found and to send us images of the said wreckage.

This was because we needed to view the photos just to ascertain the genuineness of such claims before we could make a decision. However, they told us there would be no pictures but urged us to meet them to go to the location instead.

It would have been a risky action to take considering that it was an area controlled by the insurgents. There was no reason for them to refuse to send us the exact location and photos of the wreckage if the wreckage was available.

Anyway, we were warned that it could be just an attempt to abduct our officers to be used as hostages in order to gain ransom from the Malaysian Government.

Until today, we have not received any further response from the said party on their claims that an aircraft resembling MH370 was found in Mindanao.

Moreover, if the aircraft was being hijacked, surely those involved would have already confessed to the crime since there would have been a motive and objective of such an action.

Chapter 4

Investigating the MH370 Debris

A Stirring Discovery

In the beginning, there were speculations that MH370 could have crashed into the ocean or been sabotaged by a third country. But if such allegations are true, where is the proof to confirm the matter?

In my opinion, the possibility of the aircraft crashing into the waters was higher, since there had been debris found and confirmed to be parts of MH370.

For that matter, an independent body known as the MH370 Safety Investigation Team has been established under the jurisdiction of the Minister of Transport.

In the event that the wreckage or a debris was found, the investigative body will have the first priority to inspect and gather any relevant information required. The most crucial items we look forward to were the black boxes.

In addition, any reports of the investigation could be released only by either the Minister of Transport or the Head of the Investigation Team. As a matter of fact, the investigators selected to join the team also had their backgrounds checked and were appointed by the government.

If the black boxes were to be found, we will source all avenues to retrieve them. We have identified a laboratory that is internationally recognised belonging to a neutral country to analyse the black boxes and the debris found.

What matter most is, if the wreckage is found, we will focus initially on the cockpit. We would like to know who was in the cockpit, how many

To the French Department of Justice in Paris with HE Tan Sri Ismail Omar, The Malaysian Ambassador to France.

people were in it and whether there were one or two or more persons. The next item to focus on will be the black boxes.

In all honesty, finding out the truth may not be easy as the black boxes in particular the CVR could only record the actual communication inside the cockpit during the last two hours of the flight.

As the MH370 flight was proven to continue flying for about seven hours after the turn back, the last two hours should enable us to know if the pilot/pilots were still alive and talking until the end of the flight. There was also a possibility of a third person with them in the cockpit. Sadly in this case, the audio recordings at the crucial flight phase, i.e. before, during and after the turn back, had been auto-deleted.

For the record, at the time of writing this book, there are 27 pieces of possible debris of MH370 that had been found. Three of them have been confirmed to come from MH370.

The first MH370 debris found was a wing component known as the *flaperon*. It was found in July 2015 on the island of La Réunion, a French Territory in the Indian Ocean.

Dealing with the French Judiciary

After the finding of the flaperon on the island of La Réunion, I immediately contacted the French Bureau d'Enquetes et d'Analyses (BEA) [Bureau of Enquiry and Analysis for Civil Aviation Safety] due to the fact that La Réunion island is a French territory. We did not want to prolong the matter any further and requested for BEA to let us retrieve the said component as soon as possible.

However, they informed us that the case was not under the jurisdiction of BEA but under the purview of the judiciary, i.e. the French Department of Justice.

It was perplexing to me as to why the French judiciary should be involved in this. Nevertheless, we explained that we would be going to La Réunion island to inspect the flaperon and to determine whether or not it belonged to MH370.

To that, they requested us to acquire permission from the Judge who was leading the investigation. Despite our insistence that it belonged to Malaysia and that we had the right to see it and bring the flaperon home, they asserted that it was not as simple as that.

"So, what should we do?" I asked.

They replied, "Can you come to France? To Paris?".

I agreed to fly to Paris to see them immediately. Joining me in the said mission was a team consisting of MH370's investigation officers, MAS aircraft maintenance engineers and a Legal Counsel from the Attorney General Chambers (AGC).

We departed to Paris on Thursday and arrived the next day. We then met the Judge leading the investigation and finally understood what actually happened.

We were informed that among the passengers on board MH370, there were three French citizens who were family members of an important and renowned conglomerate in France.

The family members were not happy with the update on the investigation and thus decided to conduct their own investigation. They hired their own private investigator to carry out the investigation on the incident. Through their own investigation, the family came to believe that there were elements of terrorism involved in the disappearance of MH370.

To allege that it was linked to terrorism, they had to present the result of their investigation as well as their evidences to the Judiciary's Counter Terrorism Court.

Although France has its own Counter Terrorism Investigation Department, the court had decided not to get involved since the event did not occur in the country, thus the case was rejected.

However, the family then proceeded to file an appeal, which was later accepted by the court. Because of that, the French judiciary in the Counter Terrorism Department had to reopen the case.

Reopening the case meant that they had to conduct their own investigation which was done by the Judge himself. The Judge had to appoint his own technical investigation team. The investigation team members were not from the BEA.

This technical investigation team was led by a flight Captain from Air France, and he reported directly to the Judge.

In pursuant to the French legal system as there is an ongoing investigation on MH370 conducted under the French judicial system, all the evidences found in the French territories belonged to the French investigative body, and this included the flaperon that was found in La Réunion Island.

Investigation of the Flaperon in France

Upon my arrival in Paris, I was asked to go to the Palace of Justice. I had the chance to meet with the investigation officers before I was called into the Judge's chamber.

Before entering the court, I noticed there were a lot of media personnel around the place. I was told that they will be reporting the news in the local newspaper and on television.

Before entering the Judge's Chambers, the Judge informed us only the Malaysian Government-appointed persons could be present. I was then called in as one of the representatives together with another officer from the Attorney General Chambers of Malaysia, two officers from the Malaysian investigation team, and another representative from MAS.

Together with the Judge at the meeting were the French Prosecution team and their Investigation Team.

The Malaysian Ambassador to France at that time, HE Tan Sri Ismail Omar, was also present at the court. Unfortunately, he was unable to attend the meeting because the Judge decided there were already sufficient representatives from the GOM.

I went to see him afterwards and apologised for the inconvenience. He told me not to worry and said that he understood the French protocols. Because of that particular incident, we became friends and remain so until today. Anyway, we really appreciated his sense of responsibility to make his presence there.

The Judge as the Head of the French Team briefed the meeting in French, and the meeting was translated into English by an official translator. The Judge started by officially briefing us in detail on the French Legal Systems on Anti-Terrorism, its relations to the disappearance of MH370 and the current suit on the matter in the French Anti-Terrorism Court (as described above).

The Judge then informed us that they had indeed found the flaperon. However, it had since been taken to Toulouse where it was then kept inside a special lab under tight security under the control of the French military.

They stated that the investigation is required to be done under closed-door conditions with only limited number of the relevant approved personnel. He assured us that the box containing the flaperon had not been opened yet.

We were also informed that we could only travel to Toulouse on Wednesday as the investigation will only be done on Wednesday.

To me, it was quite frustrating as we were directed to be in France to carry out the inspection of the flaperon as soon as possible.

They told us that we had to wait for the Head of the Technical Investigation Team (a flight Captain with Air France), who had to be present at the lab during the investigation.

As it turned out, the Head of the Technical Investigation Team had already flown to the US for work-related matters, and we had to wait for him to return to France.

On Wednesday, 5 August 2015, upon reaching the lab, we were subjected to a very tight security check before going into the complex.

Apart from the French and Malaysian officials, also in attendance were representatives from the NTSB US, Boeing, ATSB Australia and AAIB UK. We were briefed on the procedures for the inspection and investigation of the flaperon.

They were extremely strict on the safety and security protocols. This was evident during the opening of the box that contained the flaperon. We were not even allowed to take any photos. However, they did let us write notes on the inspection. All photographs were taken by their official photographer.

As all of us stood surrounding the box, they announced to us that the box had not been opened by showing the seals around the box and that all of us there had to bear witness to that. The box was only opened after we concurred.

When the box was opened, it contained only the flaperon and nothing else. We went around and inspected it to see if there was any evidence that the flaperon was indeed from MH370. Our initial focus was to look for a decal inscribing the part and the serial number of the flaperon. Unfortunately, the decal was detached.

We then noticed there was an indication of a repair made on the flaperon. The engineers from MAS confirmed that the repairs were indeed made by MAS and that the flaperon was from a Boeing 777 aircraft.

We also noted that the manufacturers' batch number was inscribed on the spar of the flaperon.

What is noticeable on the flaperon was that there were barnacles on the surface of the flaperon. This indicated that the flaperon had been in the ocean for a long time.

Experts at the site confirmed that there were no other records of a Boeing 777 aircraft that had crashed into the sea. The above findings were considered sufficient evidence for us and the experts present to substantiate that it was indeed a flaperon from MH370.

Following the investigation, I immediately contacted the Minister of Transport, since it was my responsibility to inform him of all the updates every four hours. I then told him that we had all confirmed that the flaperon came from MH370.

Back in Malaysia, the Minister reported the findings to the Prime Minister, who then held a press conference regarding the confirmation at 2 a.m. Malaysia Time (MYT).

Unfortunately, we discovered a different decision was made in France but was not informed to us.

While watching the news on French television about the confirmation, we also watched the news from Malaysia via the internet at the same time. Indeed, the news in Malaysia confirmed that the flaperon came from MH370; but in the BBC World News, the French stated that they will not able to give the confirmation as yet.

Oh, brother. What is it now?

I was later informed that the French did not want to confirm it as they planned on investigating the manufacturers' batch number on the flaperon first. They wanted to do so not with Boeing, but with the manufacturer of the said flaperon, a Spanish company called CASA.

I immediately contacted the French investigators and requested them to expedite the process. However, it was the summer holidays in Europe, and CASA was closed for the holidays. They would only report back to work two weeks later.

But when I arrived in Paris from Toulouse on Thursday morning, I realised there were several missed calls from the Minister of Transport. When I called him back, he expressed his surprise over the confusion concerning the flaperon and asked me how such a thing could happen.

I explained to him that all of the experts present at the investigation had actually discussed with the Head of the French's Technical Team and agreed to conclude that the flaperon came from MH370. However, we were not informed that the French authority had decided to postpone their decision until they receive confirmation from the manufacturer of the flaperon.

The Minister then directed me to see the Judge who was leading the investigation to hear his explanation.

I was scheduled to return to Malaysia on Thursday afternoon because my son was getting engaged on Saturday night.

Oh dear! I sat for a moment. It would be sad if I could not be there for my son's engagement ceremony.

But no matter what, I still had to do the job as it was my responsibility to solve the issue to the best of my ability.

So, I then contacted the French Counter Terrorism Department for an appointment with the Judge. This was no easy feat, especially when we were in a foreign country. However, with the help of the Malaysian Ambassador, I finally managed to speak with the Judge on Friday morning.

I told the Judge that I had to see him so that we can discuss the flaperon confusion. I stressed to him how important it was for me to solve the issue as soon as possible.

He was surprised upon hearing my request as it was Friday and he was heading back to his home outside Paris. It is normal for them to live outside the city, especially during summer.

But I finally succeeded in getting him to see me before midday, even though he was a bit reluctant. As soon as we met, I immediately asked, "How did this happen?".

His response was, "Don't worry. You have done your part. I have done my part".

He explained that the French had no issue with our decision to make an official confirmation regarding the flaperon even though they themselves were not ready to do so. He said that our two countries were facing different situations.

However, he seemed disappointed about the mix-up, and instead asked me how it happened. I told him that the Head of the French Technical Team and those in attendance initially agreed to the flaperon confirmation during our discussion at the lab.

It was only after everybody had concurred that I went and informed our government in Malaysia about the flaperon being confirmed as a part of MH370. He finally accepted my explanation, and the issue was considered closed for both nations.

Happily, two weeks later, they finally confirmed that the flaperon belonged to MH370.

For the record, the French still refused to return the flaperon to Malaysia, since investigation files were still open as the investigation filed by the next of kin is still ongoing.

In accordance with the French Legal Systems, whatever evidence related to MH370 that had surfaced or found within their territories shall belong to the French Government. That is the reason why we could not bring home the flaperon until today.

The earlier-mentioned incident caused me to miss the flight home to Malaysia on Thursday and I had to request from MAS to assists to arrange for another flight home. I finally got a seat on Friday via Air France flight.

I arrived in KLIA on Saturday afternoon, while my son's engagement was to be held that very night.

A lot of people at the event wanted to know more about MH370, but none of them knew that I nearly missed attending my own son's engagement because of the flaperon issue.

Even now, when I think about it, I still can't believe that I was able to solve the problem in a short time. This was really divine help.

Investigating the Flap in Tanzania

Another MH370 debris was found in Tanzania and was revealed to be from an aircraft wing component called a flap. When we were told about the discovery, I immediately ordered my officers to coordinate to bring back the said component.

This particular flap was about 10 ft in length, with a width of about 4 ft. It was much bigger than the flaperon found in La Réunion. We were informed that there were no identifiable markings. However, from the images sent to us, we were convinced that it was from MH370.

After obtaining the approval from the Ministry of Transport, I immediately dispatched an officer to Tanzania. Although the whole process was not as complicated compared to our experience with the flaperon in France, we were still met with an obstruction.

Of course, we didn't have any problem getting the green light to bring back the flap to Malaysia as the Tanzanian civil aviation team had no interest in the whole event. But the problem arose from trying to actually bring it home as we discovered that the flap was actually quite massive and weighty in nature.

As soon as our representatives arrived, they immediately inspected the said debris. Following a thorough inspection and investigation, it was confirmed that it was a component of MH370. The verification was made after the team noted the serial number that was engraved on the flap and verified with MAS aircraft record.

Unfortunately, problems arose when they arrived at the airport. The Tanzanian Customs prohibited repatriation even though it had already been packed, bound and gone through the process of delivery.

The Tanzanian Customs stated that they wanted to know the value of the item in the box so that they could tax it, even though the content had no commercial value. It was a piece of evidence to the MH370 case. It was valuable because it could help with the investigation into the disappearance of MH370.

I was in The Hague, the Netherlands at that time to attend a meeting on MH17. Coincidentally, a global meeting among the Directors-General of Customs was also held in The Hague at the same time. The Malaysian Customs Director-General at the time was Datuk Seri Khazali, so I went to see him for the purpose of seeking his assistance in the matter happening in Tanzania.

"Don't worry", he said. "I will go and discuss with their Customs DG".

As it happened, the Assistant Director-General of Tanzania was also at the meeting. In just a short period, Datuk Seri Khazali sent me a message telling me that the issue with the Tanzanian customs had already been resolved and we were able to bring home the flap with no more problem.

The MH370 Debris

At the time of writing, several other components of the aircraft have been discovered. In addition to the flaperon found in La Réunion and the flap in Tanzania, several other possible parts belonging to MH370 were also found in the coastal areas of east of South Africa, Mozambique, Mauritius and Madagascar.

Until today, 27 pieces of debris were found, and three of them were verified to have come from MH370. The three components are right flaperon, left outboard aft flap section and right outboard flap.

As most of the debris were found on the eastern coastline of the African continent, there were calls from various bodies including the next of kin, requesting for the Government of Malaysia to comb the said coastline for more debris. We did contact some of the countries in the region and were notified that it was not advisable to do so. The reasons given were that the coastline was very long, parts of which were only accessible by sea, with some stretches being inhabited by hostile groups. Therefore, it would require Government to Government Agreement and armed escorts. For the above reasons, we did not proceed with the mission, but were given the assurance from the related countries to inform us of any new findings.

There was an American man by the name of Blaine Gibson who used his personal savings to search for any debris in the area. He did it on his own accord out of curiosity to find the truth on what had actually happened to MH370 and its passengers. As an individual, he did not need to get official approval to access the areas mentioned. He claimed to have found 20 possible MH370 debris which were handed over to the Malaysian Government. One of the debris found was verified to have come from MH370.

In his search, Blaine Gibson also found a number of personal effects, such as bags, shoes and bits of clothing, which were also handed over to the Malaysian Government. However, none of the items have been confirmed to come from MH370.

All of the debris found have already been brought back to Malaysia and are now kept in a vault at the Ministry of Transport, which acts as a store for all evidences collected. These parts have to be stored carefully because in the event the wreckage of MH370 is found, the investigation has to be reopened.

The last search operations ended on 28 May 2018. As previously conveyed by the Malaysian Government, any search operations will only be resumed if there are new and credible evidences found.

However, with no new credible clues to show us where the wreckage was located, the Safety Investigation Report dated 2 July 2018 and released on 30 July 2018 remains as the final investigation report to date.

Analysis of the Debris

A team of Australian experts from the Commonwealth Scientific and Industry Research Organisation (CSIRO) had conducted a deep analysis using a replica of a flaperon from Boeing. The analysis was performed using the said replica to determine how the MH370 flaperon had resurfaced and washed away by the waves of the Indian Ocean.

In this research, CSIRO stated that if the flaperon was truly found in La Réunion, they would be able to analyse where it actually originated. It was based on this research that CSIRO published a report titled *The Search for MH370 and Ocean Surface Drift* dated 26 June 2017. The said report was then used to determine the location of MH370.

Another group that was working on an analysis of the MH370 location was the MH370 Search Strategy Working Group (SSWG), which utilised the satellite communication (SATCOM) data from Inmarsat as well as the aircraft performance data taken from Boeing. Members of SSWG consisted of ATSB and Defence Science and Technology (DST) from Australia, NTSB and Boeing from the US, UK's AAIB and Inmarsat, Thales Group from France, and DCA Malaysia.

This particular group, through ATSB, released a series of reports regarding the search of MH370, including *MH370 — First Principle Review* dated 20 December 2016.

These were the reports that Ocean Infinity had used as a reference in their search to find the wreckage.

We also agreed on the authenticity of the reports and for them to be used in the MH370 search operation in the Indian Ocean by Ocean Infinity. This was because we did not want an operation that was conducted aimlessly and without clear direction as it would only become a wasted effort.

All other debris were also investigated and analysed, however there were not enough information that can determine the cause of the accident.

The analysis of the fragments also served as a reference to locate where the search area was originally located. Unfortunately, the search came to no fruition till to date.

Chapter 5

The Media and the Shaman

Experiencing Media Scrutiny

When it comes to facing the media, both local and international, I have to say that it was an experience that I will never forget.

I have to admit that dealing with the media could sometimes be very stressful as they were constantly pressuring us for information on the latest development. But I do understand their importance since they are the ones who connect the people handling the MH370 case with the masses both near and far. This was especially true since such a case that had never happened before and had marked its own record in the history of world aviation.

Almost all of the biggest media companies congregated in the Sama-Sama Hotel, KLIA Malaysia, especially in the first two weeks of the incident, to find out more and to continuously dig for more information on the whereabouts of Flight MH370. It was as if we were hosting a major world event like the Olympics or the FIFA World Cup.

Of course, when such an unprecedented incident happened and there were no records already in place to be followed, the situation was initially chaotic and disorganised.

It was really rather challenging facing hundreds of reporters without any information or exact details about what had actually happened, especially when there were unsubstantiated stories and conspiracy theories spreading around which worsen the situation further. At times, it became really tough that the stress felt overwhelming, not just to me but to my team and others who were involved with the case.

But in the end, with the experience we gained, we were able to control the environment. At the same time, we tried to give our best in communicating with our media friends who were always anxious for the latest updates.

Since the very beginning — particularly during the first half-an-hour of the press conference held on 8 March 2014 — reporters were already flooding us with questions. Things became much more challenging three days into the disappearance as more and more information came to surface including the details about the passengers.

Every morning in the MH370 operations room, we would gather to discuss the updates and latest information. Such updates would subsequently be shared with the media during the press conference.

As the days went by, more and more information and stories surfaced some of which that we ourselves found difficult to comprehend or share because there was also some baseless stories involving the missing aircraft.

Sometimes, the media also requested for sensitive information, for example, the flight captain's history and whether or not he had any malicious intent in flying the plane to an unknown destination.

Such questions were difficult for us to respond to as we were not privy to such information as these were still under investigation by the relevant authorities. We were accused of hiding the evidence when in truth, we ourselves needed more information and verification from other related agencies.

It was imperative for us to sit down and analyse all this information so as to ensure they were substantiated by solid evidence. Only then would we release it to the media.

For the very first press conference, the ones involved in facing the media were only us from that DCA and officers from MAS. At the point of time, the Acting Minister of Transport was attending a retreat outside Kuala Lumpur.

Without any prior experience in handling such a major scale crisis, we suddenly had to face the challenges of dealing with the international media. It was a rather daunting task for us in determining what we should do in handling such heavy media attention.

In addition, we did not have enough information on what had actually happened. What we had in hand was just basic information about the missing aircraft and the captain's last words.

Initially we felt pressured to share any information received immediately with the media. Sometimes due to time constraints, the information may have not gone through adequate verification from relevant sources.

Nevertheless, in many cases, we could not arbitrarily inform the media and answer all their questions. Whatever we could share, like details about the search operations or the methods used in the mission and the results that were obtained, we readily did so.

At one time, some confusion arose because there were other government agencies which were making their own press statements which was done outside the official MH370 press conference.

The situation subsided when the Acting Minister of Transport, Datuk Seri Hishammuddin Hussein, took the lead during the press conference and was supported by MAS CEO Ahmad Jauhari and myself. He was indeed very experienced in handling the media. And by then we were more experienced and confident when facing the media.

Though the international media came duly prepared with researched information when they posed their questions to us, we decided to verify the authenticity of such information before giving them our answers.

The Foreign Reporter Who Followed Me

I recalled an interesting incident which happened to me during this period. We were staying in the Sama-Sama Hotel, KLIA, in one of the rooms prepared for us. It needs to be noted that the hotel was also scrambling to arrange accommodation for everybody involved in the incident at the time due to the sudden spike in demands and allocation of rooms was done randomly.

My room happened to be on the same floor with some of the members of the media and not with my team.

One night after work, as I was walking back to my room, I did not notice a female reporter was following me. When I unlocked the door to get in, she tried to enter the room as well. I was shocked, to say the least, especially when the reporter gave the excuse that she wanted to have an interview with me and get some exclusives.

I kept churning out one excuse after another to prevent her from getting into my room. I even told her "I will not give you any information".

Still, she insisted to get into my room for an interview, stressing that she wanted some scoops and whatnots. There I was emphasising my refusal and telling her that there was nothing that I could share with her.

She kept saying "I want to ask you something". We were going back and forth for some time until she finally relented.

Although there were many reporters who wanted to get an exclusive interview with me, there was one person whom I regarded as a "special case". We met for the first time when I was staying at the Royale Chulan Hotel. He then visited me at my office for a one-on-one interview.

That person was Richard Quest, who is a CNN journalist who works as the media Aviation Correspondent. When we met for the interviews, he was always focused and understood what we were facing due to the fact that he himself is knowledgeable on the subject of aviation.

Stalked by a Woman

One night sometime in May 2014 following a post mortem meeting after the daily press conference, I went back to my accommodation at the Seri Pacific Hotel accompanied by two of my officers, tired, hungry and in need of rest.

As soon as I arrived at the hotel, I stood in front of the lift and waited for it to open so that I could return to my room. Standing near me waiting for the same lift was a Chinese woman in her 40 s (probably with Chinese citizenship). She was wearing a hat and was holding a paper bag in one hand and a paper umbrella in the other.

It was usual for my officers to go straight to the restaurant for dinner after a meeting, but that night they decided to wait and even went inside the lift with me. The woman also did the same, and before it closed, two other security officers from the hotel got in as well.

It didn't strike me as odd at all, because occasionally these hotel security officers would make the rounds. So as soon as the door opened, I casually got out and began to walk towards my room.

Suddenly, I heard a commotion behind me in front of the lift. I saw that the hotel security as well as my own officers were apprehending the said woman to prevent her from following me to my room.

One of my officers shouted "Dato', return to your room. We'll handle this".

Without further delay, I immediately went to my room unlocked my door and kept myself safe inside the room.

About half an hour later, one of my officers called me and said, "All clear. You can come down. We'll explain everything to you downstairs".

I immediately went down to the restaurant, not just for dinner but to also find out what actually happened. That's when the hotel security officer explained to me that the woman in question had actually been seen hanging out at the lift lobby for a long time, maybe more than an hour, seemingly waiting for someone.

When asked, the only thing she said was that she was waiting for a friend. The security officer added that since they couldn't just send her away, they decided to watch her instead.

After being caught by the officers, the woman was taken downstairs and was asked to leave the hotel. However, she was still adamant about staying, stressing that she was waiting for someone.

It really had taken them a while to make her leave. It was only after they threatened to call the police that she finally yielded. We did not know what the motive was for the woman wanting to meet me or even what was actually inside the paper bag.

The next day, a different woman escorted by two tough-looking bodyguards came to the MH370 operation room asking to see me. Fortunately, I had my hands full presiding over the HLTTF meeting at the time.

My officers asked them to wait for a while. But since it took some time before the meeting ended, they decided to leave without any message.

Those were some of the interesting happenings that I had faced while leading the search operations of MH370.

Facing the Media from China

On the matter of cooperation between Malaysia and the People's Republic of China (PRC), it was quite complex because most of the victims of the tragedy were citizens of China. Overall to me the cooperation between China and Malaysia in handling MH370 was very good.

China was more focused on the treatment towards the next of kin due to the fact that 152 of the 227 passengers on board MH370 were its citizens.

All this while, we were of the notion that the victims did not have a lot of family members and that there might be only one or two children for each family aside from the parents. However, when the tragedy struck, there were a lot of people coming in and admitting to being the next of kin. Thus, in the initial phase, there were a lot of family members who got involved including in-laws and other relatives.

Most of them wanted to be included as well, so we agreed to let MAS deploy its officers to handle all briefings and clarifications involving the next of kin. We decided that one victim would be represented by four close relatives. Only they will be allowed to attend briefings and to receive updates. It would be rather overwhelming to us if we did not limit the numbers.

Personally, I think MAS had done a good job in handling all their responsibilities from relaying information about the disappearance, arranging counselling for the next of kin, as well as handling the demands made by the victims' families in addition to other responsibilities.

In the context of our relationship with the Chinese media, it was also much easier and less challenging compared to others. Apart from news of the search operations and investigations of the MH370, their questions were more direct and revolved around the treatment and welfare towards the next of kins.

We were informed that there were irresponsible parties who tried to sensationalise the situation while making up issues which were non-existent, for example, on allegations that the Malaysian Government was hiding vital information on the incident.

In most cases, the Chinese Government gave us the freedom to do our job. The support that their government gave us and the minimisation of their media's interference helped a lot in easing our persistent efforts in finding the plane whilst at the same time handling matters pertaining to the next of kins.

Offers to Find MH370: Shaman and Psychic

Throughout the period of investigation, there were various offers coming from different kinds of people offering their assistance in finding the missing flight MH370.

Indeed there were so many of them.

Once, there was a man with the title *Datuk* who brought a shaman to see me. They told me that they could find the aircraft for a certain amount of remuneration, and that the fee could be paid later.

The remuneration they sought from us was around RM 5 million. "We could have a verbal agreement" they said and that the payment could be made after the wreckage was found.

It was a weird request that I was stunned.

There was also an offer that came from India. The person in question sent me a series of emails alleging that he knew where the wreckage was. But when asked, he insisted on seeing me first.

One day he came to my office and told my officers that it was necessary for him to see me on one to one basis. The problem was that I could not do that since it was a requirement for an officer to be with me while I was carrying out a crucial task.

So I brought him into the meeting room, laid out the world map, and asked "Show me the location of the aircraft on this map".

Instead of answering, he told me "It cannot be like this" and refused to show me anything. Though he was probably a psychic, but when it comes to such matters, we needed clear facts in order for us to act.

Another incident involved a man from Vietnam, who also tried to help us. One day, I received a call from the Vietnamese Embassy in Kuala Lumpur. The caller said "I got one of my people here who wants to see you regarding MH370".

He then explained that the man had a message that needed to be conveyed to me from a monk of a temple in Vietnam.

At that time, members of the HLTTF Team had moved the operations centre to the Royale Chulan Hotel in Kuala Lumpur. The man and his friend had travelled to Kuala Lumpur and paid for their own flight tickets.

He came to see me accompanied by an officer from the Vietnamese Embassy in Kuala Lumpur and brought with him an envelope that was to be opened in front of me.

The envelope contained a yellow coloured card resembling a wedding invitation card. There was also a red ribbon inside. The card had a hand drawn map of Southeast Asia with an X marking at a spot north of Sumatra island. The Vietnamese man said that the monk told him that at the point marked X was where the aircraft had crashed.

Anyway, we had already conducted our search operations in that area including the location marked X, but nothing was found.

What was interesting was that the man did not request for anything from us, not even a fee nor compensation. I still remember his words.

"We don't want anything from you because we are really happy that we can meet you on this matter".

We were really moved by his words. At the very least, he and his friends were sincere in their quest to help us in their own way.

Aside from the above, I was also once directed by a person of high ranking position to pay a visit to someone who lived in Gombak, Selangor. I was asked to go and meet this person early in the morning at dawn. An SUV was dispatched to take me there and then send me back.

The person I was asked to meet asked me why I was there even though I think he already knew. So I told him that the reason is to find out what happened to MH370 as well as the location of the wreckage.

He then opened the holy Quran and referred to several verses therein and then told me that the aircraft had indeed crashed and sunk into the ocean. Anyway, he could not give me its exact location. This was because according to him, the aircraft was pushed by the very strong undercurrents at the bottom of the ocean and its location was not static in one place.

He also mentioned that various types of people came to seek his help in finding missing items including missing persons. He had no problem finding those that were missing on land and managed to locate them with the help of the Quran. He stressed that he could only do so if the item lost is on land because on land he could pinpoint the exact location or address of the missing items or persons.

But when it came to items lost at sea, it would be difficult for him to locate since there was no "address" in the sea. I asked him if he could give me the longitude and latitude of the aircraft's location. He again told me that it could not be done because the location of the wreckage kept changing due to the strong under currents.

Also, he said that there were no reference of latitudes and longitudes mentioned in the holy Quran.

Chapter 6

Next of Kins: Acceptance of the Tragedy

Declaring the Crash of MH370

On 29 January 2015, on the instruction of the Malaysian Government, I made the declaration that MH370 had crashed into in the southern part of the Indian Ocean and that all the passengers and crew members were presumed dead.

The decision for the declaration was discussed and agreed upon by all the Transport Ministers from China, Australia, and Malaysia.

The main objective of this announcement was to facilitate the compensation arrangements for the next of kin, in the hope of assisting them to move on with their lives.

It was not an easy task getting the consensus from all three countries when it came to the contents of the actual text for the announcement, especially on the matter of translating it into different languages. The words translated into Mandarin needed to be concise and careful so as not to offend the victims' next of kin.

We even travelled to Beijing specifically to get the Chinese Government to approve our text. Even as we arrived back in Malaysia, we still received emails from them requesting more amendments. We also had to get similar approval from Australia. Suffice to say, we changed and rewrote the text countless times and had probably made hundreds of amendments.

The three countries decided and agreed to appoint to make the announcement in my capacity as the Chairman of the HLTTF Malaysia and also as the Director-General of Civil Aviation Malaysia.

Declaration that MH370 had crashed in the southern Indian Ocean.

We initially planned to make a live announcement directly to the world on the day of the chosen date, but then noted that several next of kins were already at the venue where the announcement was going to take place. They probably came after we relayed to them through MAS that we were making a special declaration on 29 January 2015.

We considered the sensitivity and grief experienced by them, some of whom could have still nurtured some hope that their loved ones are still alive. Therefore, to prevent any unwanted incidents during the pronouncement, we decided to cancel the live announcement and aired a prerecorded televised version instead.

There were multiple reactions as soon as the pronouncement was aired on Malaysian television. Some viewed it negatively, while others were positive about it.

As mentioned above, the declaration was important and needed to be done so that the process for the next of kins to obtain commensurate compensation would be made easier, enabling them and their families to move on.

Reaction from the Next of Kins

All matters relating to the victims' next of kins were handled by MAS. The airline had provided its own counsellors to handle the situation. In addition, the Ministry of Health also assisted by providing similar services to the next of kins. But in the case of MH370, it was much more complicated because the aircraft disappeared and could not be found. Thus, without any closure, counselling and consultation became a long and winding process.

It could have been different if the plane was discovered despite the crash. At the very least, there would have been some sort of closure. But this was not the case at all with MH370.

The first week of counselling was helpful to the next of kin, but when the same issues were raised and talked about in the second, third, and fourth weeks, even the counsellors found themselves battling with pressure.

These counsellors ended up needing counselling for themselves. They felt empathetic towards the family members and gradually developed stress from the pressure.

We have to understand the position of everybody who was involved including the counsellors. What more advice could they give when there was no more solution to the problem? While at the same time, the victims' family members were getting more desperate and depressed with the pressure that they were facing.

In addition to the counselling, we also provided briefings and explanation to ambassadors of countries that were affected by MH370. As I said, it would have been easier if there were an actual conclusion. But eventually there was nothing new on the information we could give them.

To say that everybody, particularly the next of kins, was receptive and able to accept the situation at the time would be a lie. Some were aggressive towards us, accusing us of not doing our job or that we were not good enough. Some claimed that we were hiding the truth, while others stuck to their own theories about the case.

During one of the briefings we had with the next of kin, one of them approached us and expressed disagreement with what we had done. The family member said that they had heard a theory saying that another aircraft that was following behind MH370 actually shot the plane causing it to crash into the sea.

While he was aggressively relaying his thoughts and ideas, the man suddenly pulled something out of his trousers pockets. Due to the strained environment, everybody at the briefing thought the man, who was coincidentally a police officer, was trying to pull out a gun.

It turned out to be a mobile phone.

There were also some family members who insisted that the aircraft was hijacked, even though they were unable to prove it with any evidence. These were only theories that they have read in the media, especially in the social media. When we told them that all of that information was just theories, they accused us of hiding facts and did not give them clear information.

Among other things raised during that time was the question regarding compensation, especially for the next of kin of MAS employees. On this particular subject, MAS took over the handling of this matter since they were well versed with the terms and conditions of compensation for their employees.

Another issue of concern was that which involved family members of the pilots. We were worried that they would become victims of accusations that could turn extreme and dangerous. Upon the advice of RMP, information about the pilot's family members was kept away from the public.

The concerns that were raised were without solid evidence to confirm what had actually happened to the aircraft. Thus, there was a possibility that some parties, including the media, might find reasons to link the tragedy to the pilots.

All decisions that we made were to prevent the emergence of any speculations that could eventually invite anger, especially among the next of kins. This was due to the fact that a lot of theories had been created and gone viral. Sometimes, these theories were too ridiculous and extreme that they could do nothing else but hurt the families.

There were a lot of other things that could affect the next of kin. For example, when we found a possible debris of the wreckage, these conspiracy theorists seemed to enjoy speculating and questioning things like "How did it get there?" and "How were you certain that it belonged to MH370?".

Another subject that went viral was pertaining to the location where MH370 ended. We really paid a lot of attention to this information, but we could only accept those that were clear and credible and analysed by recognised experts.

Nevertheless, these speculations will continue to resurface. Until today, new theories and speculations continue to be created and end up going viral.

Reaction of the Next of Kins from China

Following the tragic disappearance of MH370, the Chinese Government made a request for MAS to brief the next of kins in Beijing. In some of these sessions, some senior officers from the Malaysian Government were also asked to attend when required.

When the briefings were done in Beijing to explain the situation to them, some of these family members refused to believe nor accept our explanations.

It was challenging at first since there was not much development in the search that we could share with them. Soon after, representatives of the Chinese next of kins requested to come to Malaysia so that they can directly listen to the briefings from the Malaysian Government. I was also asked to lead the said briefings. While in Malaysia, the next of kins were receptive and accepted our explanation without much questions or objections.

This type of positive response was different from the briefings that were held in Beijing by MAS and the senior officers from the Malaysian Government. They were inundated with many questions and, at one point, the family members became aggressive and began throwing all kinds of objects at our officers.

No matter what had transpired, I regarded them all as part and parcel of our job. There were numerous of accusations and blame that came our way. Anyway, we took everything in our stride because we believed we really had to understand and consider their feelings even though some of the accusations were unfounded.

We strived to give them the best whilst adhering to the international guidelines on handling victims of aircraft accidents.

There were times when the Chinese next of kins were dissatisfied with the explanation given by the airline and wanted clarification from the authorities instead. Despite the challenges, we tried our best to fulfil their requests to the best of our ability.

But of course, handling matters concerning MH370 was no easy feat. One has to understand that such a tragedy has never occurred in the history of world aviation. There were no precedence for us to use as reference.

Instead, the handling of this tragedy will become the standards and reference that will be used and followed in international protocol in the future.

PART II — MH17

Chapter 7

Tragedy Strikes Again

Another Tragedy

The shooting down of Flight MH17 in Ukraine on 17 July 2014 was the second devastating tragedy that I had to experience as the Director-General of the Department of Civil Aviation (DCA).

The MH17 incident was a shock to us all. Even I found myself horror-stricken upon receiving the news, especially since it was only months after the disappearance of Flight MH370.

Imagine, the trauma of the MH370's disappearance on 8 March 2014 had yet to dissipate, and there I was facing another tragedy involving Flight MH17 just four months later.

The news about Flight MH17 quickly travelled around the globe. As we all know, the tragedy that sparked global outrage had caused the deaths of all 283 passengers and 15 crew members of the said Boeing 777 aircraft.

The aircraft exploded in midair from the force of the air missile before it crashed near Torez in Donetsk Oblast, Ukraine, about 40 km (25 miles) from the Russian border.

Dismayed over the news, Malaysia had a special session in the *Dewan Rakyat* to condemn the uncivilised and inhumane act of terrorism by the perpetrators responsible for the incident.

According to media reports, the debris of the wreckage had scattered far and wide that it even reached the village of Petropavlovka in eastern Ukraine, which was among the locations of the MH17 aircraft fragments found by the locals.

As we all know, MH17 departed from Amsterdam Airport Schiphol on 17 July 2014 at 12.31 pm Amsterdam time (7.31 pm Malaysian time). At 4.22 pm Ukraine time (10.22 pm Malaysian time), MAS confirmed that it had received an update from Ukraine's Air Traffic Control saying that they had lost contact with Flight MH17 i.e. 30 km from waypoint TAMAK around 50 km from the Russia–Ukraine border.

International news reports also mentioned the discovery of aircraft debris near the village of Hrabove, Ukraine — a rebel-controlled territory near the Russian border. Satellite images showed wreckage, dead bodies and personal belongings scattered for several kilometres.

I still remember that when the tragedy struck, Datuk Seri Liow Tiong Lai had just been appointed as the new Minister of Transport Malaysia two weeks before. One of his first tasks was to meet the Transport Minister of the People's Republic of China to discuss on MH370.

It is already noted that Malaysia had a Tripartite Agreement with China and Australia in the search of the missing MH370. Thus, at the time of the crash, he was actually in China preparing for the meeting with the Chinese Minister of Transport to discuss matters regarding MH370 search operations.

While Datuk Seri Liow Tiong Lai had already gone one day before me, I departed for Beijing on the evening of 17 July 2014. When we arrived at the Beijing Capital International Airport at 12.30 am, we saw that several Beijing Airport representatives and MAS officers were already there waiting for us.

I was surprised that they were there to welcome us. One of the officers asked us to step aside and gave us boarding passes to return to Malaysia on board the same aircraft.

I initially thought that they had cancelled the meeting in Beijing. But even if they did, why wouldn't they let us spend the night in the city when we were already tired from the long flight? Moreover, why did they cancel the meeting in the first place?

However, the officer told us that something had happened in Kuala Lumpur and showed us the news on his phone.

Flight MH17 crashed in Ukraine!

I was stunned and groped to understand what had actually happened. So I switched on my phone. Again, lots of unread messages began coming in. Then my wife called me to inform me of the news.

By then, the Transport Minister had already been informed of the incident and was on his way to the Beijing airport. We then had a discussion about the tragedy that struck MH17 and the possibility of it being shot down by a missile.

He instructed us to return to Kuala Lumpur to obtain more detailed information and to discuss our next course of action.

Coincidentally, the tragedy occurred during the fasting month of Ramadan. Our flight to Beijing departed from KLIA at 6.30 pm. We had to break our fast (*iftar*) on the aircraft and ended up having our pre-dawn meal (*sahur*) on the same aircraft.

We arrived at KLIA early Friday morning and immediately went to the MAS Operations Centre where we were briefed about the MH17 tragedy. It took us a while to decide on the next course of action. The biggest issue at the time was that nobody was allowed to enter the location of the crash site.

The CNN network somehow managed to air extensive coverage of the scene of the accident site which clearly showed the wreckage of the aircraft with bodies scattered around the area.

We agreed that our main mission would be to enter the crash site immediately for initial investigation due to the fact that the aircraft belonged to Malaysia. The meeting decided that a special task force should be sent to the site to bring home all the victims.

After the meeting, we attended a briefing to the next-of-kins of the victims including flight and cabin crew family members. A sombre and sorrowful atmosphere enveloped the meeting, especially when the *Eid al-Fitr* was just around the corner. The more heart-wrenching realisation was that all the passengers and crew involved were killed in the tragedy.

The family members wanted to know the date we could bring the bodies home. They also wanted to know what actually happened and requested to be brought to the crash site as well. The minister explained that we would do our best to arrange to transport the bodies home as soon as possible.

The next day, we were instructed by the Prime Minister to travel to Ukraine to determine what could be done there. As soon as we received the order, we immediately departed to Kiev, Ukraine, via Amsterdam.

As soon as we arrived at Amsterdam Airport, Schiphol, we immediately attended a meeting with MAS officials who had just landed from Kiev.

They informed us that it was near impossible to enter the site of the crash because the area was under the control of rebel groups which were in conflict with the Ukrainian government. Therefore, we had to re-strategise our plan to resolve the said problem.

Retrieving the Black Boxes

The first problem that we faced as soon as we were told about the tragedy that had befallen MH17 was finding ways to retrieve the black boxes and bringing out all the victims from the area.

We were able to gather some information at that time through the CNN's network that reported about the surrounding where the bodies were found scattered around the crash site.

Fortunately, the separatists had done nothing untoward following the crash, and they were surprisingly very respectful towards the bodies found in the area and made attempts to cover them. They also set aside the bodies that were found, although they did not make any attempt to bring them out of the crash site.

At the same time, the Malaysian Government discreetly sent several officers led by the National Security Council Assistant Chief Secretary Colonel Mohd Sakri Hussin to retrieve the aircraft's black boxes after the Malaysian Prime Minister obtained the rebel leader's agreement to handover the CVR and FDR to our commandos. The leader of the rebel groups, Mr. Alexander Borodai, also happened to be their Prime Minister.

Therefore, on 21 July 2014, Col. Mohd Sakri as the Chief Negotiator led a team of 12 commandos known as *The Dozen Persons* managed to successfully obtained MH17's black boxes as well as the bodies of the victims after negotiating and obtaining the agreement of Mr. Borodai in Donestk, Ukraine.

This was a tremendous success achieved by Col. Mohd Sakri and his team despite its confidential and risky nature. I was really impressed and proud of the resilience and bravery shown by these men. Malaysians should be proud and thankful for their commitment and bravery in successfully negotiating with the separatists to bring out the bodies and the black boxes from the crash site.

While the team was making the effort through negotiations with the separatist we were ordered to wait in Kiev. We were then informed that the black boxes were safely retrieved and would need to be transported with the bodies by rail to the city of Kharkiv immediately.

The journey was at night and took about eight hours to reach its destination. On our part, we monitored its movement through continuous communication. At one point, we lost contact but fortunately managed to get back online after one hour.

We were also told that as soon as Col. Mohd Sakri and his team arrived at Kharkiv, there were other parties demanding the black boxes as well, which included the Ukrainian authorities as well as several foreign authorities/agencies. They attempted to get the black boxes in any way they can, be it voluntarily or by force.

Fortunately, the colonel and his team managed to block such attempts and successfully delivered the "precious and vital" equipment safely.

The Ukrainian Government through their military also confronted our team of commandos and tried to force them to hand over the black boxes, stressing that all the evidence related to MH17 should be surrendered to their government.

However, Col. Mohd Sakri was adamant in ensuring that the black boxes were delivered to me and subsequently to the MH17 investigation team.

Our team of commandos were successful in fending off the efforts made by the Ukrainian Government despite the latter's attempt to force the team into signing a transfer document that was written in the Russian language.

I was in Kiev during that period and had remained in contact with our officers in Kharkiv. Subsequently, I was directed to go to the Netherlands Embassy in Kiev to await the black boxes.

We did not actually know how the black boxes were to be transported from Kharkiv to Kiev at the time, but were directed not to use the main road as there was a possibility of another party blocking our path in an effort to seize the device.

I did receive several calls from our Minister of Transport, who was in Amsterdam awaiting the bodies in Kharkiv to be transported to Amsterdam. He instructed that I brought the black boxes out of Ukraine as soon as possible.

I was then informed that our team of commandos were successful in bringing MH17's black boxes back to Kiev on board an aircraft courtesy of the United Nations (UN).

I was rushed to Kiev International Airport to receive the said black boxes. As soon as the flight from Kharkiv arrived, a feeling of relief washed over me. I was at the Kiev Airport's VIP room where the black boxes were officially handed to me by one of the commandos, Major Mustapha. He carried the black boxes in a backpack. We were informed later that the backpack never left him until the items were given to us at Kiev airport.

The black boxes in question consisted of the CVR and the FDR. CVR is a device that records the communication between pilots, the interaction between the pilots and the air traffic controllers, as well as other sounds inside the cockpit, while FDR records amongst other things, the aircraft flight path, speed, altitude, engine performance, aircraft configurations and systems.

As the representative of the Malaysian Government, I then officially handed over the CVR and FDR to the Netherlands Ambassador in Ukraine. This was due to the fact that the Netherlands was leading the technical investigation into the crash of Flight MH17. We have agreed that the black boxes be sent to the AAIB at Farnborough, UK, for the preliminary analysis.

Without further delay, we immediately boarded a special executive aircraft dispatched by the Belgian Air Force and departed to Farnborough, UK, at about 11 pm. On the flight, together with our Malaysian team (which comprised of an investigator and an engineer from MAS) were also representatives from the Netherlands, the UK, the US, Ukraine, and Australia as well as representatives from the ICAO. We placed the black boxes in the middle of the aircraft in full view of all the delegates.

However, we were suddenly informed that the aircraft would land at the Brussels International Airport and that we were to be transferred to another aircraft. The switch had to be made because the pilot's flight time limitation was about to expire.

At the Brussels Airport, we boarded another Belgian Air Force aircraft, C-130 Hercules. We also placed the black boxes in the middle of the aircraft in full view of all the delegates.

In the UK, the aircraft landed at an Air Force airbase located north of Farnborough because the Farnborough Airport was closed due to operational night curfew.

Following immigration and customs clearance, we boarded a special bus to Farnborough. Our bus was escorted by police vehicles at the front and the back.

While we were in the middle of our journey, the bus was suddenly stopped by one of the escorting vehicles. A police officer then came out to ask the bus driver to drive faster. In jest, the bus driver said that it was the first time in his life that a police officer had told him to drive faster!

We arrived at AAIB around 5 am and were immediately taken to the lab for a briefing about the protocols in handling the black boxes.

As a formality, the AAIB officials then asked all the delegates if the black boxes that we had brought with us were the same ones that the Malaysian Government retrieved from Kiev before being handed over to the Netherlands Government.

Since everybody replied in the affirmative, we were asked to sign an agreement stating that the black boxes were indeed genuine. The AAIB official jotted down the black boxes' serial numbers, placed the black boxes inside a safe, and took several photos of it.

All of the delegates concurred that the safe was empty prior to the black boxes being placed inside it. The safe was then locked with one of the keys being kept by AAIB while another was given to a representative of the Netherlands' investigative body. The door of the safe was then sealed to further ensure its safety and security.

After it was safely placed inside the safe, all parties involved were asked to sign a form to show their consent with the protocols.

We were already tired by then and went straight to the hotel to rest.

Back at the hotel, I was informed that the bodies of the MH17 victims had been flown to Amsterdam, Netherlands, to undergo the Disaster Victim Identification process.

The Difficulties of Entering the Site

Back to the beginning of the time when the news of MH17 being shot down was received, we were directed by the PM to rush to Ukraine to obtain the latest information as well as to arrange to bring back the bodies.

From KLIA we landed in Amsterdam and continued our journey to Kiev. Upon arrival at Kiev, we were greeted by a Ukrainian Minister and escorted to meet the Deputy Prime Minister of Ukraine. Our team consisted of the Minister of Transport YB Dato Sri Liow Tiong Lai, the Chairman of MAS Tan Sri Md Noor Yusof, the Malaysia Ambassador to Ukraine HE Chuah Teong Ban, the officers of the MOT, and myself.

Sadly, we were not welcomed with open hands by the Ukrainian Government, and were told they could not ensure our safety during our time in the country. In a news conference held after the meeting, we were asked about Malaysia's next step in resolving the issue. The Minister of Transport responded that since MH17 was registered in Malaysia, we would make an effort to assist in the investigation and do our best to get access into the crash site.

To clarify, it was extremely difficult for our team to enter the site of the crash, especially when it was controlled by separatists who were in conflict with the Ukrainian Government. Even the Ukrainians themselves were not able to access the site.

In our courtesy call to the Deputy Prime Minister of Ukraine, our Transport Minister requested for assistance in getting the approval for our Malaysian investigation team to enter the site of the crash. The DPM, however, informed that he could not even guarantee us our safety in the country, let alone enter the crash site.

Fortunately and by coincidence, our Foreign Minister Datuk Seri Anifah Aman was also in Kiev for a bilateral discussion on the handling of MH17 at the same time. He suggested that our Transport Minister meet with the members of the Organization for Security and Cooperation in Europe (OSCE) to get the approval for the Malaysian investigation team to gain access to the site.

OSCE was initially reluctant to allow us access into the location on the grounds that it was an active conflict zone where separatist forces were "at war with the Ukrainian Government". We were told that there were not only one separatist group in the area but seven groups in total.

Nevertheless, the Transport Minister did not relent and continued to press for urgency for the investigating team to immediately enter the accident area in order to inspect the scattered debris of the wreckage. It was crucial for us to have video recordings, photographs and notes taken of what was in the area to be used as evidence before they were all removed, destroyed or even tempered with by irresponsible parties.

If such an event were to happen, then there would be great possibility that the evidence of the actual cause of the accident would be lost.

After hearing the request made by the Transport Minister, the OSCE stated that they would need to get the approval from their Headquarters in Brussels. They requested that we return to see them the next day.

When we arrived at the OSCE office the next day, the first question they asked was about a Malaysian team that was already at the location of the crash.

"If a Malaysian team is already there, why do you need to add another?".

To be honest, we were baffled by that particular information. We were only allowed to go to the location after the Transport Minister denied the presence of the supposed Malaysian team at the crash site.

However, the approval also came with several conditions that only three of us from Malaysia could access the site within the time frame fixed by the OSCE. The movement schedule was so tight that we were expected to keep to the time frame as there were possibilities that the separatists could stop the team from entering the area.

After much discussion, we agreed on the three officers who would be going to the location. Two of them were DCA officers: Captain Philip J. Selvaraju a pilot and airworthiness engineer Mohd Naemy Fahmy Mustapa. The other person was Azhari Mohd Dahlan, the MAS Director of Engineering and Maintenance.

The way they entered the crash site reminded me of a James Bond movie. They had to fly to Kharkiv the next day and be greeted by an OSCE official upon arrival at the airport where they would spend the night at a prearranged hotel.

The following day, the team would depart for Hrabove early in the morning at a given specific time in a vehicle driven by a different OSCE officer. As soon as they arrived at Hrabove, they would be taken to the site of the crash but would be stopped at several roadblocks by various different separatist groups. However, the OSCE has already prearranged for the separatist groups to let them proceed to the site.

Thankfully, they arrived at the site all safe and sound. However, the original two-day mission was later extended to one more day due to the expanse of the area.

Meanwhile, all of us in Kiev were waiting anxiously with bated breath. We could not help worrying because they informed us through phone calls that they could hear bomb explosions and gunshots everywhere throughout the inspection. They could also hear similar sounds at the hotel where they spent their nights in Donetsk, which was already a ghost town at the time.

In order to enter the crash site, they had to ride in an armoured bulletproof four-wheel drive vehicle while being escorted front and back by similarly armoured military transports.

The Malaysian investigation team was the first technical team to enter the crash site. During their three-day mission, the team received extensive coverage from international media.

Among the findings found by the investigation team were a large number of debris and fragments of the aircraft scattered in a large area. The most significant finding was that the distance between the location where the cockpit crashed and the other main parts of the aircraft was very far, about 6 km apart. They also found signs of fire at the midsection of the aircraft.

The above findings indicated that the aircraft had exploded in mid-air whereby the cockpit section crashed first and followed by the other parts of the aircraft. The fire occurred around the area of the fuel tank which could have exploded and burnt as it crashed to the ground.

The said discovery further reinforced our view that MH17 could have been shot.

The DCA investigation team's preliminary report, which also included several pictures taken in the area, was handed over as critical evidences to the Dutch Safety Board (DSB) which was leading the technical investigation of MH17. The report was later used as a basis for our briefing presented to the Prime Minister.

The picture on the cover of the DSB's Final Investigation Report was an actual picture taken by the Malaysian investigation team.

According to Annex 13, in the event of an aircraft accident, the country of occurrence is responsible for the investigation of the accident. This means that Ukraine should have been the country to take the lead.

However, the Ukrainian Government was unable to do so because the accident occurred in an area which was under the control of the separatists group for which they had almost no access at all. Thus, Malaysia and the other countries involved in the investigation agreed that Ukraine delegated to the Netherlands to lead the investigations.

This was due to the fact that Flight MH17 departed from Amsterdam, most of the victims were Dutch citizens, and the Netherlands is not far from the site of the accident. However, Malaysia being the State of Register and the State of Operator remained an integral member of the investigation team.

Given that the MH17 incident was a complex case that could have involved the shooting down of a civil aircraft by a missile, it was necessary to conduct an extremely detailed investigation. In addition, this high-profile accident involved various countries, therefore accredited representatives from the relevant countries were needed to be invited to join the accident investigation team.

In the case of MH370, Malaysia led the investigation and the accredited representatives were from seven countries. These representatives were from China, Australia, France, Singapore, Indonesia, the US, as well as the UK.

However, in the case of MH17, the Netherlands led the investigation with six accredited representatives, which consisted of Ukraine (State of Occurrence), Malaysia (State of the Operator and State of Registry), the United States (State of Design and Manufacture of the aircraft), the United Kingdom (State of Design and Manufacture of the engines), Australia (State that provided information and photos at the scene), and Russia (State that provided radar information as well as air traffic communications and information on weapons' systems).

This particular investigation was technical and conducted in accordance with ICAO Annex 13 whereby the main objective of the investigation was to find the cause of the accident and to ensure that a similar accident will not recur.

On the other hand, the second investigation was a criminal investigation. It was also led by the Netherlands. Other members of the team were countries of interest such as Malaysia, Australia, Ukraine and Belgium (to fulfil EU requirements).

The appointment for Malaysia to join the criminal investigation body known as the *Joint Investigation Team* (JIT) was however delayed. It was said that the delay was due to Ukraine's disapproval and unhappiness over Malaysia's effort to negotiate with the separatist group in order to retrieve the black boxes and the bodies.

Malaysia had explained that we negotiated with the separatist group under desperate situations as we wanted the black boxes and the bodies of the victims to be retrieved immediately. The bodies of the victims needed to be identified and preservation measures should be carried out before handling over to prevent decomposition.

Chapter 8

A Rather Impossible Mission

Repatriation Process of the Remains

The Malaysian Prime Minister decided to dispatch a delegation to negotiate with the rebels in order to obtain the black boxes as well as to bring back the remains of the victims.

It was a fact that the process of recovering the bodies of the victims was extremely risky and complicated. Col. Sakri, who led the mission to Ukraine, not only managed to bring out the black boxes but also succeeded in retrieving victims' remains as well. The remains were transported to Kharkiv by rail.

Family members and relatives of the victims were already waiting patiently for every single news and development of the incident. We did not want to leave the bodies out there for too long a time to prevent deterioration as well as anxiety to the next-of-kins.

The train embarked on its journey at night, travelling from the site in Hrabove to Kharkiv for about eight hours. We found out there were other parties that were also interested in monitoring the movement of the train due to the important nature of the cargo.

We even lost communication with the train for nearly an hour during the journey at one point which caused a lot of concerns amongst many, especially the Malaysian Government. This was due to the fact that we had made a great effort to ensure that the black boxes and the remains would be transported safely.

It was a big relief to many when we finally restored contact with the commando team on the train until they reached Kharkiv.

According to the plan, following its arrival the bodies would be taken straight to Amsterdam for an official identification process. However, as soon as it arrived at Kharkiv, the Ukrainian Government decided to impose the international procedure for the repatriation of the bodies. This caused the process to stagnate, resulting in a delay.

The movement of a corpse from one country to another is quite a complicated procedure as a death certificate needs to be produced for each of the deceased. But how could there be any when we had yet to even identify the bodies?

Furthermore, the process had to be implemented to international procedures, which included cleaning, drying of the body and the use of embalming chemicals. The body would then need to be neatly wrapped before it can be placed in a sealed coffin. It would be also required to have a declaration from a medical authority before the body could be exported. It is indeed a complicated arrangement.

The Ukrainian Government insisted that all such procedures were complied with before the bodies could be transported to Amsterdam. Given that this was a tragic disaster situation, how could we possibly comply with such requirements as there were more than 200 bodies to be considered and some were not in perfect condition?

With limited concessions granted by the Ukrainian Government, the process resulted in reduced time to complete; after which we were allowed to bring out the corpses out from Kharkiv to Amsterdam.

Nevertheless, praises and recognition should be given to both the Netherlands and the Malaysian teams who gave their best effort in handling the matter even though most of the victims were Dutch citizens. The two countries did their best in giving respect towards the deceased.

Upon arriving at Amsterdam, the victims were given full honours and subsequently transported to the Heumensoord Military Camp in Amsterdam for storage process and thereafter to be followed by the Disaster Victim Identification (DVI) process.

Disaster Victim Identification (DVI) Process

A tragedy such as MH17 required an extensive area for the purpose of storing the bodies and conducting the DVI process. The amount of space was not the only criterion, as the venue also had to be suitable for such a procedure. The most appropriate venue for this would be a hospital, but a hospital could only handle one or two forensic cases. Meanwhile, we had hundreds of bodies in our hands.

To ensure safe storage of the bodies, a special morgue that could house 298 bodies was needed to prevent the rotting of the remains.

The process of identifying the bodies began with an *ante mortem* process (not to be confused with *post mortem*) that is through obtaining the deoxyribonucleic acid (DNA) from the next of kins to be matched with the DNA of the deceased. This process is called DVI.

An action committee was formed to manage the DVI. The main task of the committee was to retrieve the bodies, clean them, and match the DNA of the remains with the DNA of the next of kins.

After the identification report of each victim's body was obtained, it went through a quality control process. The quality control process was carried out by another committee which specialised in ensuring that the previous process had complied with the procedures set out. Only after obtaining confirmation from the quality control committee would the identity of the victim's body be confirmed.

Once the identity was confirmed, the DVI management would forward the verification report to MAS and the embassies of the countries involved. MAS would then notify the victims' next of kins.

Some people did ask why it took so long to conduct the identification process. It did take a long time because the process required careful handling before confirmation could be made.

We did not want to make mistakes as it could complicate matters and cause embarrassment for everyone involved.

Identifying the Remains

The initial procedure was to examine the condition of the corpse. If the body was in good shape and perfect condition, then the process of identifying would be easier.

However, throughout the DVI process for the victims of MH17, only one victim was able to be identified without any need for a DNA matching. This was because an international passport was found inside the pocket of the shirt that he was wearing. The body of the victim was identified by the photograph and details in his passport. Thus, the DVI Team agreed to confirm the particular identity of the deceased.

As for process of identifying the other remaining bodies, the DVI process as mentioned earlier was done. The pictures of the body was taken first and the experts would examined any markings that could be identified.

Thereafter the examination was done with reference to dental records.

If there was no clear identification, the committee would then compare the victim's DNA with the ones submitted by the next of kins. Such comparison had to be done one at a time using the next of kins DNA until they could find a match. This particular process needed to be done thoroughly. Bear in mind, this meticulous identification process involved hundreds of bodies.

Only after the DNA matching had been completed, and the committee members had given their unanimous approval, would the DVI report confirming the identity of the body be signed. The report was then submitted to the Quality Control Committee and subjected to a thorough quality control process.

The Quality Control Committee then reviewed and ensured that the process had been done in accordance with the approved procedure.

Both processes were done thoroughly, hence the reason why the DVI reports took a long time to be completed.

Bodies of Unidentified Victims

As explained earlier, the victims' identification process took a long time. However, the team was able to complete their task with much success. In the end, only two victims were unable to be identified.

The names of the two victims were registered in the list of passengers. However, their bodies could not be found. There were several theories related to the missing bodies. Some speculated that the remains perished due to explosion/fire. Some others believed that the victims could have fallen into the nearby lake adjacent to the crash site.

However, family members of both victims accepted the matter as fate.

Managing the Bodies of Malaysian Victims

After all the victims were identified based on their countries of origin, the DVI Team from the Netherlands kept these bodies inside the mortuary cold rooms while waiting for their respective governments to claim them and subsequently brought them home.

For the 43 Malaysians that were killed in the crash, the cost of bringing home the bodies were paid for by MAS and not the Malaysian

Government. These bodies that were confirmed to be Malaysian nationals were transferred into a cold room of a morgue that had been specially rented while waiting for repatriation to Malaysia.

The remains of Muslim victims had to be bathed first followed by a funeral prayer.

According to a Malaysian *ustaz* that had been flown to Amsterdam, after the bathing and the prayer, the bodies needed to be buried as soon as possible. It would be inappropriate for us to keep the bodies for a long time after both the rituals were done. However, in these circumstances, such immediate burial could not be done.

Victims from other religions were also kept inside the mortuary cold rooms while waiting for the process of repatriation. Representatives of various religions — Islam, Christianity, Buddhism and Hinduism — were flown by MAS to Amsterdam to provide advisory services and conduct religious ceremonies according to the needs of their religions.

The Efficiency of the Malaysian Team

Meanwhile in Malaysia, an MH17 Operations Centre was established in DCA, Putrajaya, to monitor the situation in Amsterdam when the DVI was in progress. The main objective of this operation centre was to coordinate the progress of the DVI with MAS officers and the Malaysian Embassy in Amsterdam and The Hague. To provide timely communications between Putrajaya and Amsterdam, the centre began its operation at 5 pm Malaysia Time, which is 10 am Amsterdam Time.

The MH17 Operation Centre, which was jointly managed by the MOT, DCA, and MAS officials, was opened daily for the latest updates, especially on new information regarding the bodies that had been identified regardless of their nationality.

Malaysia also sent medical officers from the Ministry of Health Malaysia (MOH), the Malaysian Armed Forces, and the Royal Malaysian Police (RMP) to assist in the DVI management process in Amsterdam. Most of these medical personnel were still young.

What prides us the most was that the competencies of all our medical staff were recognised and respected by DVI experts from Europe. The experts stated that they were impressed by how our officers were very efficient, quick on their feet, and knew what needed to be done throughout the process.

Sombre and solemn moment during the arrival of MH17 victim bodies.

Sombre and solemn moment during the arrival of MH17 victim bodies.

A Rather Impossible Mission 113

Sombre and solemn moment during the arrival of MH17 victim bodies.

The fact was that these medical personnel were forensic officers who had been specifically selected and given comprehensive DVI training in preparation for the possibility of MH370 discovery. Therefore, when the MH17 tragedy struck, the team was dispatched to Amsterdam instead to assist and gain exposure in the DVI management.

These were officers who were already exposed to the task from their various assignments around Malaysia. Therefore, they were not just well-versed but well-equipped as well. In addition, the RMP had also given them training and exposure on DVI management.

The European experts were not only impressed by the fact that they had their equipments ready but also by the fact that they also had their own uniforms. Again, these were all prepared for the possibility of MH370's discovery.

Meanwhile, in the DCA Operations Centre, the seating charts of the passengers on board MH17 were displayed with emphasis on Malaysian nationals. As soon as MAS officers in Amsterdam informed that there was confirmation that the identity of a Malaysian victim was announced; we at the Operations Centre would proceed to record that information in the MH17 seating position chart.

The DVI committee in Amsterdam could only identify the MH17 victims one at a time. With this information, we at the Operations Centre were able to predict which body of a Malaysian victim would be found next according to the seating position in the aircraft. All these had been done in an organised and structured manner based on our experience in handling MH370.

As soon as the bodies of Malaysian victims were identified, MAS would proceed to inform the next of kins. In this case, our function was to assist in coordinating the efforts for the repatriation of the bodies to Malaysia.

A sub-committee consisting of officers from the MOT, DCA, MAS and MAHB together with the Armed Forces organised a ceremony with full military honours for the bodies of the MH17 victims upon arrival at KLIA. In preparation for the ceremony, training was held for a week to ensure that the bodies received with the appropriate respect. The training included the correct way of lowering the coffins from the aircraft and also the correct placements of the coffins into the hearse. Each and every coffin was draped with a Malaysian flag.

On 22 August 2014, 40 days after the tragedy, the first 20 bodies of Malaysian nationals arrived safely on board a special MAS aircraft at KLIA. The ceremony was held at the KLIA Bunga Raya Complex which was usually reserved to welcome State Leaders and Heads of Government.

The government declared the day of the first group's arrival to be the Day of National Mourning, with the ceremony aired live across the country. Everybody at the ceremony was clad in black. It was a sombre and solemn moment when the bodies arrived, and the whole country stopped to observe a moment of silence.

His Majesty the 14th Yang di-Pertuan Agong and His Royal Consort of Malaysia also graced the ceremony to welcome the bodies of the victims. Also in attendance were the Prime Minister, Cabinet Ministers, next of kins, and representatives of MAS management and staff, especially the flight crew and cabin crew.

From the KLIA, all the bodies were sent directly to their respective hometowns for the funeral ceremonies. The bodies for burial outside the Klang valley were specially flown by courtesy of the RMAF.

Similar solemn ceremonies were held soon after, to receive two other groups of bodies that arrived later on.

Chapter 9

An Unforgettable Experience

Handling the Bodies of the Victims of MH17

Among the things that I cannot forget was the feeling of sadness when the victims' bodies were identified after undergoing the DVI process. Some of them were intact while others were incomplete. Some bodies were even identified with their limbs found separately. All of them were arranged into their respective coffins along with parts of their bodies that were recovered.

There were bodies with only an arm or a leg, and we brought back to Malaysia as they were. There were also cases where we brought back one part of the body first and a month or so later, another limb was found and brought home. We also had a situation where the body was already buried after arriving in Malaysia but another body part was found soon after.

According to an Islamic Religious officer brought specially from Malaysia to Amsterdam, it was obligatory to perform all the Islamic rituals even if only one part of the body was found and identified. This included the ritual of bathing and funeral prayer followed by the burial. Similarly, religious representatives from other religions who were also specially brought to Amsterdam carried out their respective religious rites on the bodies or body parts of their followers.

That was the main reason we did not allow members of the victims' families to see the body. Not all of them were complete. The Government and MAS even advised the next of kin to instead remember the victims as they were when they were alive. We were worried that if they were to look at the bodies of the victims, they would be severely traumatised.

Nonetheless, for those whose bodies were incomplete, the family members would be informed about the condition of the body and the possibility of discovering more of them later on. This was to prevent confusion and disappointment if other parts of the body were subsequently identified and returned to be buried.

This was also because the process of matching and identification of all the limbs from the same body would take about two to three months.

As for personal belongings that were found at the scene, the task of collecting, identifying, and returning them to the next of kins went to MAS. We did not succeed in finding each and every one of these belongings, but those personal items that were found were collected and kept securely. However, there were items that were burnt or destroyed and, therefore, could not be identified.

There were family members who accepted these personal belongings graciously, there were some who were sad and there were some who did not want to accept them at all. To them, such items would only bring more sorrow since their loved ones have passed on.

Reactions from Next of Kins of MH17

In matters related to the next of kins, including counselling sessions, the responsibility and task were delegated fully to MAS. One could say that the counsellors working with MAS were severely pressured and stressed out by the need to not only handle the next of kins of MH17 tragedy but also at the same time required to also handle the next of kins of MH370 who were still waiting for updated news of their loved ones. To make things harder there was no closure for the families of the MH370 victims, whose loved ones disappeared without a trace.

When MH17 was reported to have been shot down by a missile, the incident was made public through breaking news on TV and social media. What remained unclear was the identity of the perpetrator and the reason for the shooting.

In contrast, the disappearance of MH370 remained unsolved which became the next of kin's source of depression and trauma. However, with the help of counsellors from MAS and the Ministry of Health, most of them had become more accepting of what had happened.

Some family members of the MH17 victims were more accepting of the fact that what had happened was destined to happen. However, most of them were dissatisfied and wanted to know who was responsible for the tragedy. They demanded that the parties involved to be brought before the court and punished for their crime.

What they wanted was justice for the death of their loved ones more so because of the shocking and tragic nature of their passing. If the death was caused by an aircraft accident resulting from a technical problem — like damage to the engine or technical issues related to the aircraft — they would have probably been more accepting of their loved ones' fate. But when it involved the downing of an aircraft, the next of kin's family members interpreted the act as intentional on the perpetrator's part.

The JIT had alleged that there could be Russian involvement in the shooting, but the Malaysian Government at that time, however, disagreed, citing that the evidence was not strong enough for such accusation.

In another report, the investigating team was said to have been able to intercept a phone call on the downing of MH17 between Moscow and the separatist. Again, the Malaysian Government opined that the evidence was not concrete enough.

Within the scope of the judiciary, a Judicial Action Committee comprising of five countries, the Netherlands, Belgium, Ukraine, Australia, and Malaysia, was established. One of their first options was to bring the case to the international tribunal through the United Nations Security Council.

The problem was that as soon as the proposal was tabled at the UN Security Council in New York on 29 July 2015, Russia used their veto power to reject the proposal. On the other hand, the case could not be brought before the International Court of Justice (ICJ) as well because it did not involve a conflict between nations but a conflict between individuals or a group and the country concerned.

In view of the earlier-mentioned situation, the committee decided to file the case through the International Prosecution, and the Netherlands was appointed to file the charges in the Netherlands, based on the fact that most of the victims were Dutch nationals.

At the time of writing this book, the MH17 case was being heard in the District Court of The Hague in Badhoevedorp, Netherlands, in which the Netherlands' Prosecutors filed charges against three Russian Army Officers and one officer of the Ukrainian Army. All four were alleged to have been involved in the downing of MH17. However, the case was heard without the accused being present in court — a *trial in absentia*.

Chapter 10

The Black Boxes and Why MH17?

Analysis of the Black Boxes

The journey from Kiev to Farnborough, UK, was a long and treacherous one. Our flight was directed to land in Brussels where we boarded another aircraft which later landed in a military base. We then boarded a special bus to AAIB in Farnborough where we handed over the black boxes for safekeeping. We were understandably very exhausted by the time we checked into the hotel early morning to rest.

Then, at 10 am the same day, we were gathered at the AAIB before entering their special lab where the analysis of the black boxes would be conducted.

A black box contains a digital chip that keeps all data and recordings of an aircraft while it is in operation. The chip is coated with a type of rubber material that cannot be destroyed at the time of an accident.

We were then briefed by AAIB on the procedures to be used in analysing the black boxes.

Due to the limited space in the laboratory, only two representatives from the eight countries were allowed to enter. The rest of the representatives were placed in a meeting room equipped with a CCTV which enabled them to monitor the analysis that was being done.

The representatives agreed that everyone present should be given the opportunity to be in the laboratory on a rotational basis.

Through the CCTV in the meeting room, we were able to see what was being done to the black box. It took the AAIB experts about a day to remove the CVR chip as work must be done carefully to avoid any damage. The chip was then inspected for any damage. Next, it was placed in special equipment for the purpose of downloading its recorded content. It is noted that a CVR records the last two hours of the communications in the cockpit.

The AAIB experts were the first to hear the recording before it was handed over to us. I was one of the first people to be given the opportunity to listen to the recording.

Prior to the tragedy that struck flight MH17, I have had the experience of listening to recordings of the final moments from several air crashes. In some cases, Muslim pilots were able to recite the *Shahadah*. In others, screams and cries could be heard in the recording. There were also cases where the pilots swore and cursed, while some were just stunned and speechless.

The same could not be said in the last two hours of MH17. We could hear a conversation between three people when it should only be two inside the cockpit. However, these interactions were relaxed and cordial in nature — nothing out of the ordinary.

According to the Official Investigation Report issued by the DSB, the third person heard in the conversation was a member of the flight's cabin crew.

We listened real carefully to the details of the CVR, especially in the last 15 minutes, but found nothing suspicious. In it, there was a call from the Dnipropetrovsk Air Traffic Control Centre in eastern Ukraine directing the captain to fly directly towards waypoint RND. The captain responded with compliance to the instructions. Soon after, Dnipropetrovsk Air Traffic Controller was heard again directing the aircraft, this time to head to waypoint TIKNA after RND. But it was after this that everything suddenly went quiet, except sounds that resembled a broken radio.

Representatives of the other related countries were also given the opportunity to listen to the recording. Subsequently, with the assistance of AAIB, a transcript of the conversation was written by the representatives of the two countries present. The transcript was then reviewed and confirmed by two other representatives from the other countries present.

Upon review, the CVR recording was disconnected, i.e. at 4.20.03 pm Ukraine Time, which was 10.20.03 pm Malaysian Time.

For the record, the CVR analysis took two days to be completed.

Following the CVR analysis, we then moved on to the FDR analysis.

The analysis procedure of the FDR is similar to that of the CVR. The FDR records more than a hundred technical data of the aircraft's condition, and the chip is able to record the last 25 hours of the flight.

However, in the case of MH17, it only managed to record about three hours of flight time from when it departed from Amsterdam to the time it crashed.

Similar to the aforementioned CVR analysis, AAIB technical experts first ensured that the digital chip was in good condition. As it was with the CVR, the process was witnessed by two representatives of each of the countries present.

After confirming that the chip was in good condition, the recording was then downloaded so that the aircraft data prior to the crash could be analysed.

The data recording initially indicated that MH17 was flying at an altitude of 33,000 feet. All systems of the said aircraft including the engines were in good condition, with the flight itself flying along the planned path. However, similar to what had happened with the CVR recording, the FDR recording was suddenly disconnected soon after.

Upon checking the time when the FDR was cut off, it showed 4.20.03 pm Ukraine Time, which was 10.20.03 pm Malaysian Time, i.e. the same time the CVR was disconnected.

Representatives of the countries present at these two analyses were of the opinion that the preliminary analysis showed that there was a great probability that MH17 had been shot down, considering that there were characteristics of it being shot down by a missile. The view was in line with the opinions made earlier by most aviation experts.

However, more detailed and thorough investigations needed to be done.

I, therefore, immediately contacted the Minister of Transport to provide the latest updates on the analyses of the black boxes. He instructed a detailed report to be submitted and to brief the Prime Minister, who was scheduled to be in Amsterdam on the third day of *Eid*. Since there were three days left before *Eid*, I had no choice but to celebrate the Holy Day in London in order for me to prepare the reports for the Prime Minister.

On the third day of *Eid*, as scheduled, we went to Amsterdam and met with the Prime Minister the following day to update him on the matters of the MH17 tragedy.

MH17 Possibly Shot Down?

I flew to Amsterdam on the third day of *Eid*, and on the fourth day, I proceeded to brief the Prime Minister on the updates of our findings before the press conference.

The briefings included the analyses on the black boxes, where the delegates of countries involved concurred it was highly probable that the plane was shot down. However, a detailed investigation needed to be conducted. I also briefed him of the findings from the preliminary investigations done by the three Malaysian officers who went to the site of the crash.

The Prime Minister expressed his agreement with the opinion regarding the downing of the aircraft. He agreed that the incident was out of the ordinary and needed to be investigated in detail to get to the actual cause of the crash.

He subsequently expressed a similar notion at the press conference, while I gave a brief explanation of what we found and heard in the CVR and FDR recordings.

The Malaysian Government at that time was also concerned with what had happened, especially since it occurred in the month of Ramadan just before *Eid* celebrations. The next of kins wanted the bodies to be returned before the holy celebration, but it was not something that could be done easily due to the complications surrounding the process of finding, gathering, and identifying the bodies.

The experience that I gained from handling both cases of MH370 and MH17 taught me a lot of new things that were out of the ordinary, especially in handling bodies of the victims, since as it not only involved the sensitivity of the family members but also because both were very high-profile cases.

Why Shoot MH17?

Many were of the opinion that MH17 was shot down by the Ukrainian separatist who had the support of the Russians, while others believed that they were aiming to shoot down the aircraft carrying the Russian President Vladimir Putin himself, as both MH17 and the President's aircraft apparently look the same from ground level.

The question has been: Why would they want to shoot someone who was supporting them?

There were also claims that MH17 had actually entered a no-flying zone. But the fact of the matter is that there were other flights (reportedly

60 of them) traversing the zone on the same day. On the day that MH17 was shot down, there was an Air India flight AI113 flying from the opposite direction towards the west, whilst another aircraft, a Singapore Airlines flight SQ351, was behind MH17 both heading towards the same direction.

We were informed that there was an earlier occurrence whereby a Ukrainian military aircraft was shot down in eastern Ukraine. However, the Ukrainian Government did not close the entire eastern area of the Ukrainian airspace but instead issued a notice that an aircraft should not fly below 30,000 feet. When MH17 was shot down, it was flying at an altitude of 33,000 feet and was not anywhere near the limited zone with the height limitation.

Although we did not find anything suspicious in both the early CVR and FDR recording analyses, we did note that the two recordings were disrupted at the same time. This indicated that the aircraft system was disconnected simultaneously and that an explosion had most likely occurred causing the entire aircraft system to abruptly stop working all at once.

The discovery of several pieces of debris by the Malaysian investigators at the crash site further fuelled our beliefs that the aircraft had been shot down. This included a large number of debris of aircraft parts scattered over a very large area indicating that the aircraft had exploded in mid-air.

The report of the Malaysian Investigation Team at the site was submitted to DSB Netherlands that led the MH17 technical investigation. Many of these initial investigation findings became the basis of the Preliminary Report by the DSB on 9 September 2014. The photographs taken by Malaysian investigators at the site were also used by DSB in the said report.

The official report on the downing of MH17 was issued by DSB in October 2015, more than a year from the date of the incident. The report took some time as DSB was only able to enter the accident area to retrieve the fragments and debris of the aircraft for detailed analysis four months after the incident.

In their report of the investigation, the DSB provided detailed explanations regarding the cause of the incident, i.e. the report stated that the left side of MH17's cockpit exploded from the blast of a missile 9N314M-model warhead which was carried on a 9M38-series of missiles installed on the BUK surface-to-air missile system (BUK is a Russian word for "beech", i.e. type of tree). Also, in the final report, the DSB stated that MAS was not to blame and that there was nothing wrong with the way that MAS operated the aircraft.

Chapter 11

Forensic Investigation

MH17 Detailed Investigation

Each and every aircraft accident requires extremely detailed investigations. These investigations are usually divided into two areas, i.e. technical investigation and criminal investigation.

The *technical investigation*. This investigation analyses facts and evidence for the main objective of identifying the true cause of the incident. The investigation must abide by the procedures as stated under Annex 13 and has to be conducted by an independent body.

A technical investigation does not aim to find the perpetrator(s) but focuses only on finding the cause and doing in-depth analysis to ensure such an incident will not be repeated in the future. Safety recommendations will also be stated in the final report as a means of improving the safety standards of civil aviation.

The *criminal investigation*. This investigation focuses more on finding and determining whether there were heinous acts done towards the aircraft, like sabotage, hijacking, shooting down and many more. More often than not, a criminal investigation is carried out by the police and the justice department of the country where the incident happened known as the State of Occurrence.

These two branches of investigation are conducted separately, led by the State of Occurrence.

As a reminder, technically, Ukraine should have led both the technical and criminal investigations in the case of Flight MH17. However, they did not do so due to the fact that the Ukrainians were unable to enter the site of the crash.

Therefore, Ukraine delegated to the Netherlands to lead the MH17 investigation instead. This was not only because most of the victims were Dutch nationals but also because the Netherlands is also much closer to Ukraine compared to the other countries involved. For the same reason, the Netherlands was also appointed to lead the criminal investigation through a group known as the JIT.

It was noted that the Dutch investigating body, i.e. the DSB, was supposed to go to the site of the accident to inspect the wreckage, take pictures of the area and retrieve debris of the wreckage from the site to be analysed for the purpose of finding the cause of the accident. However, the Dutch Government was only allowed into the accident area four months after the incident.

As for Malaysia, at the request of the Transport Minister, a three-person Malaysian investigation team was given permission to enter the site. Our team was the first technical team to enter the crash site to take pictures and conduct preliminary investigations (including identifying the debris). However, despite being permitted into the location, we were still not allowed to remove anything from the site of the crash.

One after the other, all the evidences were carefully analysed for the effects of shots, burns, explosions and cracks.

The black boxes at that time had already been analysed at the early stage by the AAIB UK. The analysis was then forwarded to DSB Netherlands for detailed investigation.

All of the debris of the wreckage from the site were identified and recorded based on the original position of the parts on the aircraft. Next, the debris were reassembled to resemble the shape of the original aircraft. The whole process was like putting together a jigsaw puzzle. Investigators would then inspect this "reinstalled plane" to find the effects of bullets, shots, explosions, burns and cracks. The investigation would then be focused on these effects, whether they occurred before, during, or after the plane crashed.

Such work was done thoroughly and carefully.

Each and every aircraft equipment that was collected from the crash site including the engines were also carefully inspected to detect if there were any damages that might determine the cause of the accident. The investigation also focused on whether or not the damage occurred before, during, or after the plane crashed.

Additionally, the team also analysed the injuries that could be detected on the victims. Similar to detailed operations performed on the aircraft debris, a thorough examination was also conducted on the victims' bodies to analyse the effects of bullets, explosions, burns and common injuries.

Radar recordings were obtained from the Ukraine and Russia ATC centres for analysis of any irregularities of the MH17 flight prior to the crash.

All findings related to the investigation were then recorded and discussed to determine the cause of the incident. When necessary, the team would consult the manufacturers of the aircraft and aircraft equipments for further clarification.

Responding to Accusations

In the early stages of the investigations, we started with assumptions on the cause of the accident. However, such assumptions were made based on the evidence that were analysed. Thereafter, we looked for and gathered stronger evidence to strengthen the assumptions.

The Final Investigation Report issued by the DSB dated October 2015 stated that MH17 shattered in mid-air while traversing the airway of eastern Ukraine on 17 July 2014. Further comments from the report pointed out that the plane was hit by an explosion from a missile on the left side of the cockpit. The missile 9N314M warhead was fitted on a 9M38 missile system which was mounted on a BUK surface-to-air missile. All 298 passengers and crew were killed in the incident.

The DSB report mentioned the cause of the crash and listed a number of safety recommendations to ensure that such an incident could be avoided in the future. No charges were filed.

Thereafter, the criminal investigation process proceeded to become more active. With the cause of the incident already established, it then became necessary to find the evidence on who was responsible for the downing of the MH17.

While waiting for the black boxes to be brought to Kiev, the Ukrainian Ministry of Foreign Affairs had summoned the Malaysian Ambassador, HE Chuah Teong Ban, to Ukraine to hear Ukraine's Government side on the matter. Since I was directly involved in this case, I was invited by Ambassador Chuah to accompany him.

The Ukrainian Government conveyed their dissatisfaction over the effort of the Malaysian Government in dealing with the rebels. To them, the negotiation with the rebels seems to indicate our recognition of their movement.

As a representative of the Malaysian Government, Ambassador HE Chuah explained that the Malaysian Government dealt directly with the rebels only to bring out the black boxes and the bodies of the victims so that they could be managed and handed over to their next of kins.

Chapter 12

Media Reactions and Response

In Media Attention Again

The announcement on the downing of the MH17 was made by the Ukrainian Government. This was due to the fact that such an announcement should be made by the State of Occurrence.

Meanwhile, here in Malaysia, the media were more focused on getting clarification from MAS, DCA, and the Minister himself about the incident and our next course of action. We were also without much information. Therefore, we needed to dispatch a special team to Ukraine in order to obtain accurate and up-to-date information and to also assist the Ukrainian Government in handling this tragedy.

On the part of the western media, most of them did not point fingers at Malaysia for what had happened. They were more sympathetic about the tragedy and were interested in finding the identity of the perpetrators and/or the party responsible for the tragedy. Some accused the Ukrainian rebels of shooting down MH17, while others pointed their fingers at Russia. However, there were also those who accused Ukraine of perpetrating the incident. The media insisted on digging deeper into finding the mastermind and the culprit behind the missile.

From the initial stages of the MH17 incident, we were of the opinion that there was high probability that the aircraft had been shot down by a missile. This was also the opinion of international aviation experts around the world based on the wreckage and debris which were strewn over a very wide area. These were also shown on the mainstream media across the world and in social media, unlike MH370 of which the disappearance still remains a mystery.

A lot of people accused Malaysia of hiding the truth of what had happened to MH370. There were others who insisted that what had happened to MH17 had also happened to MH370. It really was tiring to debunk all these theories, especially when some of them were too ridiculous to even be considered.

On the other hand, there was another group of people who despite previously being enraged by the MH370 tragedy suddenly became sympathetic towards Malaysia in the case of the MH17 tragedy.

This came as no surprise because, in the space of just four months, our country had to face two major incidents involving two aircraft of the same type, the B777, and operated by the same carrier, MAS.

Effect on MAS and Malaysia's Reputation

It could not be denied that the image of MAS and Malaysia's reputation, in general, were deeply affected due to both MH370 and MH17 tragedies. We decided that what we needed to do was to evaluate the situation in a bigger picture.

There were some who criticised MAS with the sole objective of bringing down the airline. There were also reports that had gone viral listing MAS as one of the ten most dangerous airlines in the world.

It was quite strange to accuse MAS as one of the ten most dangerous airlines because there was no apparent technical issues involved in both tragedies. In the case of MH370, the aircraft went missing without a trace, while MH17 was shot down. How could such accusations be directed to MAS and the Malaysian Government? Nothing negative was recorded pertaining to the operations and maintenance procedures of both aircraft in the investigation reports. Aircraft operations and maintenance are the two most important pillars in aviation safety.

Yet, Malaysia also received many praises for continuously striving to find the solutions in resolving the two cases. The Minister of Transport, accompanied by a Task Force, had made a courtesy visit to the US Department of State at the White House in Washington DC. He also visited his US counterpart, the Secretary of Transportation. The purpose of the visit was to explain what really happened and to brief them on Malaysia's efforts in preventing the two tragedies from happening again.

During the visit, the US Government acknowledged Malaysia's efforts and promised to provide the necessary support for what has been undertaken by the Malaysian Government.

From Washington DC, we then headed to the ICAO Headquarters in Montreal, Canada, whereby our Transport Minister was given the honour to speak at a special event session of the ICAO Council presided by the President of ICAO himself. The Minister emphasised that in the case of MH370, there was a need for a system that can track an aircraft location wherever it is flying.

For the record, during the time that MH370 went missing, there was already a system called the Aircraft Communications and Reporting System (ACARS) which would send a signal to airlines every 30 minutes. This communication system which functions by downloading information to the airlines such as aircraft heading, engine performance, and the status of aircraft systems is known as *Real-Time Aircraft Tracking*.

Following MH370's disappearance, the system changed its frequency of downloading interval from every 30 minutes to every 15 minutes. This enables airlines to monitor the movement of their planes more frequently.

At the same event, the Minister stressed that the MH17 tragedy could have been avoided if country facing a conflict or a war closed its airspace around the high-risk areas to ensure aircraft safety. In addition, countries that face such conflicts must report the situation to ICAO, while airlines should be encouraged to share any information regarding conflict zones. The data gathered by ICAO should then be used by airlines to make their own risk assessments. This would help prevent untoward incidents from happening as had been in the case of MH17.

The Minister of Transport emphatically ended his speech by saying "Doing nothing is not an option".

The Malaysian Government would not sit back but would continue making efforts in searching for the truth of what had happened in both tragedies.

In the case of the MH370 tragedy, for example, the Australian Government offered to lead the search operations using its own national funds. However, at one point, Australia requested Malaysia to provide financial contribution to the MH370 search effort. In appreciation of Australia's efforts, the Malaysian Government agreed to their request, in the hopes of finding the wreckage of MH370.

Millions of Malaysian Ringgits had been expended with 26 countries providing assistance to Malaysia in our search operations.

Indeed, Malaysia's image and reputation were affected due to the countless baseless theories about the two tragedies. At the same time, Malaysia also received assistance and cooperation from various countries that wanted to help solve the mysteries of aviation. What we strived for was not only for Malaysia but also for the entire aviation industry worldwide.

Chapter 13

Social Media and Conspiracy Theories

Social Media Theories

All information regarding the downing of MH17 which were received from the media (including social media), were closely monitored as it could in some way assist us with the investigation.

However, first and foremost, they needed to be assessed and verified the validity of the information especially on social media.

In seeking for the truth of what really happened, we required the evidence that was found in the accident site, for example, debris from wreckage, Cockpit Voice Recorder (CVR)/Flight Data Recorder (FDR) recordings, air traffic records and many more. We needed actual proof rather than haphazardly accepting anything that had been broadcasted and made viral.

If you were to watch television programmes, particularly the news and dialogues with these "experts" of civil aviation, all kinds of theories came out every day. Some ask the government to look at the issue from this angle or that.

However, what was the basis of these supposed experts' theories? How can there be suddenly so many experts who knew everything about civil aviation, aircraft, and air accident investigation?

We tried our best to watch the news and read the views/reviews that were viraled. Sometimes we did not have much time due to work constraints, but we would attempt to save the programme to look at it at a later time.

We noted that many of the reports and theories presented were unfound and could not be used directly. In fact, some of the theories were even quite ridiculous.

Happily, there were also some local aviation experts who knew what they were talking about. Their theories managed to help the public to understand the real situation and provided the investigators with some valuable thoughtful insights.

Some international NGOs were of the opinion that the shooting down of MH17 was due to geopolitical conflict. I once attended an international NGO briefing on the topic of the above allegations. However, what was shown as evidence had been taken from news and internet reports and not from original reports or publications from recognised bodies.

Anyway, we should not allow for justice to revolve around the mainstream media and social media platforms; neither should we allow manipulations of information by any parties as it could hurt the families of victims who are still grieving the loss of their loved ones in the MH17 tragedy.

Dismissing Conspiracies

There were actually several theories about what had happened to MH17.

What was clear was that the aircraft had been shot by a missile. But who was the perpetrator? Some theories alleged that it was committed by Russian-sponsored rebels. But why would they shoot a Malaysian aircraft?

To us that could only be a theory. The Malaysian Government could not say with confidence that Russia was to be blamed in this case. A statement from the Malaysian administration at that time gave a firm picture that there was no solid evidence to accuse these pro-Russia rebels.

The result of the technical investigation revealed that Flight MH17 had been shot down by a 9N314M missile carried by the 9M38 series missile system attached to the BUK surface-to-air missile system. But no one, whether it be the rebels, the Ukrainian military nor Russia, confessed that they were involved in this incident.

According to sources, there were rumours that the plane had been shot down by separatist groups based on a post written by Igor Strelkov, a commander of the Donbas People's Militia, on the social media site VKontakte (VK). In it he wrote that they had already given out a warning: Do not fly in our "air space".

The posting made a mention about an AN-26 transport aeroplane owned by the Ukrainian military that was allegedly shot down and crashed near a mine in Torez, the same city where MH17 had crashed.

The posting was later removed when Igor Strelkov found out that it was said that the plane they had shot down was not a military aircraft but a commercial one.

Ukraine's Crisis Media Centre surmised that the separatist groups might have mistaken MH17 as a Ukrainian military aircraft. But so far, this theory has not been confirmed, even though the possibility is high.

However, these theories that concerned MH17 focused more on whether or not Russia and the pro-Russia rebels were involved.

Indeed, the conflict between the two countries to some extent tarnished the investigation and stunted the process to bring the matter to justice.

In their report, the JIT investigation named four individuals who were responsible for ordering the shootings: three of them were Russian military personnel and another a Ukrainian military officer. The four accused have been arraigned in the District Court of The Hague in Badhoevedorp, Netherlands, as members of the rebels who helped arrange the installation of a Russian missile system that allegedly shot down MH17.

However, Russia had expressed disagreement with the JIT's accusation. The Malaysian Government at that time also disagreed on the basis that there was insufficient evidence. However, the prosecution went on with the indictment process.

We hope that the trial in *absentia* that is currently ongoing in the Nevertheless, the prosecution proceeded with the indictment process.

Chapter 14

The Final Investigation Reports on MH370 and MH17

A Summary of MH17 Investigation Report

The final report of the MH17 accident investigation titled *Crash of Malaysia Airlines flight MH17; Hrabove, Ukraine, 17 July 2014* had been released by the DSB; in The Hague, the Netherlands, in October 2015.

The above report stated that the Malaysian Airlines aircraft type Boeing 777–200, registration 9M-MRD, flight MH17 had shattered mid-air in eastern Ukraine at 4.20 pm Ukraine Time, 10.20 pm Malaysia Time on 17 July 2014.

Next, the report stated that the left side of MH17's cockpit exploded from the blast of a missile. The 9N314M-model warhead was carried on a 9M38-series of missiles installed on the BUK surface-to-air missile system.

The report also provided a list of safety recommendations to be followed by all agencies involved in the accident.

Nearly five years after the incident of MH17, the Dutch Public Prosecution Service (*Openbaar Ministerie*) filed charges against three Russian military personnel and one Ukrainian military officer who were believed to have been involved in the shooting down of MH17. If found guilty, they could face either a severe punishment of lifetime imprisonment, a prison sentence not more than 30 years without parole or even an early release.

The MH17 Accident Investigation Report, October 2015.

At the time of the writing of this book, the trial for MH17 is being heard at the District Court of The Hague in Badhoevedorp, Netherlands. At the beginning of the trial, all 298 passengers' names were read to the accused. As expected, the trial was conducted without the presence of the four accused in court (*trial in absentia*). Even though this case is going on without the accused being in court, hopefully, justice can be upheld.

A Summary of MH370 Investigation Report

The final investigation report of the MH370 titled *Safety Investigation Report, Malaysia Airlines Boeing B777-200ER (9M-MRO); March 8, 2014* was issued by the Malaysian ICAO Annex 13 Safety Investigation Team for MH370 on 2 July 2018.

It is of interest to note on page xx, para V. Objective and under ICAO Annex 13, Section 3.1 page 3–1:

> "The sole objective of the investigation of an accident or incident shall be the prevention of accidents and incidents. It is not the purpose of this activity to apportion blame or liability".

The MH370 Safety Investigation Report, 2 July 2018.

Under Section 3.2 Conclusion of the Report, amongst others, stated that:

"Without the benefit of the examination of the aircraft wreckage and recorded flight data information, the investigation was unable to identify any plausible aircraft or systems failure mode that would lead to the observed systems deactivation, diversion from the filed flight plan route and the subsequent flight path taken by the aircraft.

However, the same lack of evidence precluded the investigation from definitely eliminating that possibility. The possibility of intervention by a third party cannot be excluded either".

The Report ended with the following statement:

"In conclusion, the Team is unable to determine the real cause for the disappearance of MH370".

Closing

Maturing Through Experience

The disappearance of MH370 was a bitter experience that was difficult to forget throughout my career leading the DCA since 2007.

Personally, even though it was a bitter experience, the MH370 tragedy had to be resolved transparently and responsibly. The most important thing that I learned when facing such an event is to always try to remain patient and calm. No matter what happens, we have to keep calm.

A lot of people asked me how I managed the stress when I was dealing with the MH370 tragedy. To me, we need to always be focused on everything that we do. It is also important to be confident and assured of what we are doing. When facing a crisis, knowledge is the most important weapon to a person.

I learn new things every day. There was always something new when it came to the aviation industry. My deep interest in this field helped me to always find the latest information and ensure that I did not feel bored when asked about the same thing repeatedly. It is important to have passion and drive to continue learning and to update your knowledge when it comes to the development of the industry, not just on technical aspects but other aspects as well.

We must also be bold enough and not be afraid to ask questions, and most importantly, we must train ourselves to remain calm and patient when faced with difficulties. If you do not know something, you have to admit that you do not know. Do not allow yourself to react negatively. There will always be new things to learn every day and when it comes to

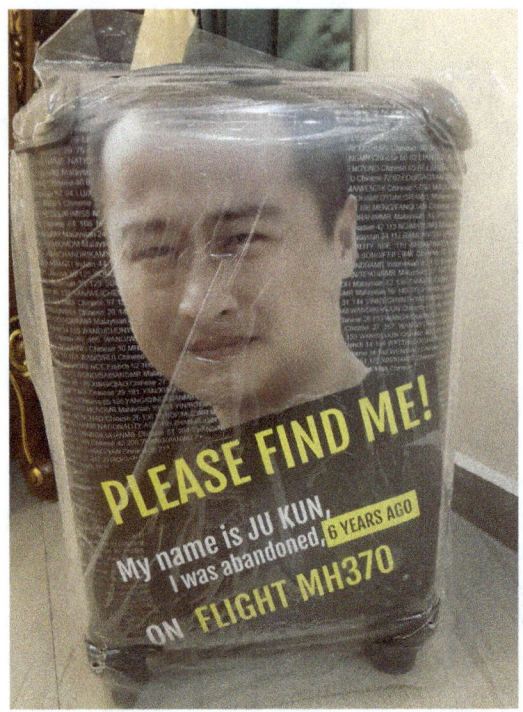

The cabin baggage as received from an unnamed next-of-kin.

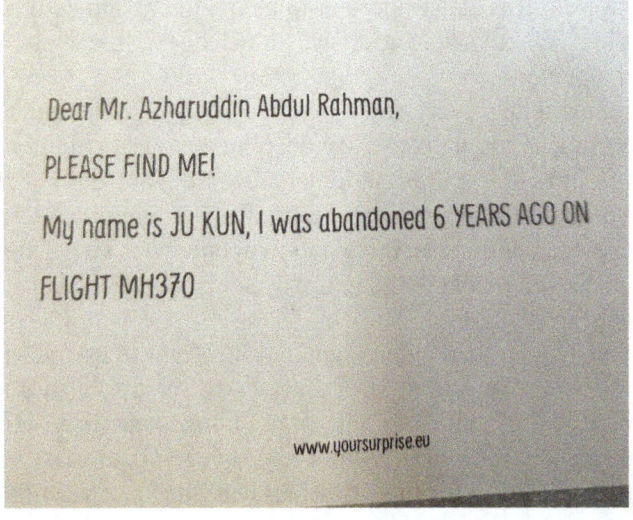

The note as found in the cabin baggage.

this particular field, you have to always be humble and prepared to learn from anybody including your own officers and subordinates.

I have to admit that the first time I was tasked with handling matters concerning MH370, the stress was overwhelming to the point that I was not able to get a good sleep. My daily life was immensely disrupted.

For three months, I was not able to go home, and for six months I was not able to return to work in my office at the DCA Headquarters in Putrajaya. For six whole months, the hotel was simultaneously my home and my workplace.

Initially, the pressure felt very heavy. I never had a good night's sleep despite being given a room at the hotel. Every day I would preside at the HLTTF meeting in the morning and attend the press conference in the late afternoon. Basic needs like eating and sleeping were no longer of importance at that time.

All that I could think about at the time was getting the latest information to relay to the next of kin, to the media, and to the public. The whole world demanded to know what had happened to MH370. I had gone far and wide, from China to Australia, the UK, France, the US, Canada, and to other countries, in our effort to solve the mystery.

Now, even after seven years, I admit that I still wish to know the whereabouts of MH370. I still thought about its disappearance even to this day.

In fact, to this day, there are still some next of kin who still find it difficult to accept the fact that Flight MH370 had ended in the ocean. This was evident when on 22 February 2020, I received a package from Brussels, Belgium.

Two weeks before that was my birthday. Therefore, when the package arrived in the mail, I thought a friend from Brussels had sent me a birthday present.

However, as soon as I opened the package, I was shocked to find it contained cabin luggage bearing a photo of a person whom I have never met. There were words written on it which read:

PLEASE FIND ME!
My name is JU KUN, I was abandoned, SIX YEARS AGO
ON FLIGHT MH370.

I decided to check the list of names of the people on board MH370 to see if there was a passenger with the same name. And there it was, Ju Kun, a 32-year-old Chinese citizen.

It really spooked me, especially since it was already close to 12 am at that time, as my family and I had just returned from attending a wedding reception.

After looking more closely at the picture, I realised that the background bore the names of the passengers of MH370. Not only that but inside the package there was also a card attached bearing the same earlier-mentioned words.

I immediately called a senior police officer about the situation, and he told me to neither touch nor open the luggage. He also asked me to make a police report the next day.

After making the report, a team of forensics police officers came to my house to retrieve the said luggage. However, upon opening it at the police station, the police revealed that there was nothing inside the luggage.

A few days later, I was notified of a new message from a WhatsApp group from someone I did not know. The message was also directed to several senior officers and reporters who were involved in the handling of the MH370 case. Just like the other receivers of the message, I decided to leave the group.

It was a shock to me to realise that the person who sent the package and the WhatsApp message knew my house address and my personal mobile phone number despite the fact that we only moved into this new house only about a year ago.

To us, this was an indication that there are family members of the victims who still believe that the passengers of MH370 are still alive to this day and want them to be returned to the family.

The tragic disappearance of MH370 remains a mystery that is still being discussed around the world with the main question being how it happened and what could be done to solve the case. But the mystery remains as a mystery.

Finding Strength Through Support from Family and Friends

Just like everybody else at the time, my family was also shocked upon hearing news about MH370's disappearance. They too asked me a lot of questions about the incident like WHY and HOW could it disappear.

The same can be said about my friends and relatives. A lot of them asked me the same questions. So I told them, just as I told everybody else, that the information that we had was very limited and there was not much for us to share. During the initial period following MH370's disappearance, even we ourselves did not know what had happened.

At that point in time, the burden of my work seemed more than heavy, so when I told my wife and children that I might have to stay in a hotel and would not be home for an indefinite period of time, they were very supportive and encouraging.

It was at that time that I could feel the importance of having strong support from family. My wife was and will always be my source of strength, who gives me an honest opinion whenever I ask her. Every time I felt down, she would be there for me. Not only did she take care of my daily needs but she also became my emotional support. When I was facing the toughest most stressful situation, she would make sure to always be there for me.

My wife used to work in a senior management position in a private company in Kuala Lumpur, so she really understood the level of commitment that I had towards facing this challenging task. Thus, when it came to all matters concerning the children at the time, I left every decision to her. Moreover, all of our kids, the two girls and the two boys were already grown up. They also understood the demands of my work, especially the fact that I was facing such a critical situation.

As the man of the house, I enjoyed taking the whole family out for dinner at least once a month. But after the MH370 tragedy struck, I was not able to do so and could only bring them to dinner at the hotel where I was staying at the time. Because of this, they probably liked it when they saw their father on television, in mass media, and on social media.

Once, my daughter told me that a reporter had asked to interview the whole family. I said no. I did not want the family to be involved in this. I was also worried that if any misinformation was given, it might give rise to negative perception.

Sometimes, my relatives and friends would ask me to clarify some of the theories that had gone viral about the case. Most of them were just theories and not supported by solid evidence. More often than not, such theories were created with imaginary evidence which seemed convincing to the general public.

When our operations centre was moved to PWTC, we were given accommodation at the adjacent Seri Pacific Hotel. One Saturday morning, I found myself with a little bit of time on my hand and was craving for Nasi Lemak Tanglin that was located close to my mother's house in Bukit Damansara.

So I went and bought *nasi lemak bungkus* (rice wrapped in banana leaf) and immediately headed towards my mother's house so that I could have breakfast with her. It had been quite a while since I saw her, nearly three months since MH370 happened.

My mother saw me from afar. As soon as I approached her, she embraced me and asked "How are you doing? Are you well?".

I felt moved. I could see that she had a lot of sympathy for me. She told me that she had been watching me on television.

I knew that my mother had always been concerned about my well-being and was aware of the development of the MH370 case. The prayers and support that I received from her, from my family, my siblings and friends were the ones that helped me a lot to become stronger and tougher in carrying out my responsibilities on the case.

Throughout that period, I missed a number of weddings of my nieces and nephews, and also events held by relatives. I nearly missed my own son's engagement. I hope that they understood my situation.

There were people who assumed that I actually knew all the information concerning MH370 but was concealing it. In truth, there was nothing for me to hide. I just didn't know what actually happened.

Even to this day, there are people who still ask me about the case. For instance, I recently attended a school reunion with my former classmates. They said that since I have already retired, I could finally share what really happened.

Support from family members and friends truly give me strength.

Support from strangers was also a very great motivation for me. At times, someone would come to me and say he understood the challenges and pressure that I was facing while giving me kind words of support and encouragement.

Even while abroad, I was greeted not only by Malaysians but also by foreigners who came to me for a chat and ask for updates on both cases.

Efforts to Transform DCA

One of the things that made me proud was when the DCA was transformed in line with the ICAO call for civil aviation authorities in the ICAO Contracting States to be made an independent body.

The transformation of DCA into a statutory body known as the CAAM was considered another milestone for the development of the aviation industry in Malaysia.

The Bill for the establishment of CAAM was passed in the final session of the Parliament in 2016, and CAAM commenced its full operations on 18 February 2018.

The establishment of CAAM was in line with ICAO's recommendation that the Contracting States establish their own autonomous authority to ensure that civil aviation safety is managed efficiently and meets the standards and recommended practices by the ICAO.

To ensure that the country's civil aviation authority is competent, efficient, assertive and trustworthy, the body must be given the freedom and support to provide up-to-date legislations as well as up-to-date technical documentation and procedures.

In terms of human resources, it must have qualified and adequate number of technical personnel. It must also be able to provide the latest training as a priority to such personnel.

The salary and remunerations scheme must be able to commensurate that of the industry. As part of the strategy to stay ahead and competent, it must have a good strategic plans and updated succession planning to ensure continuity and sustainable enforcement.

In fact, to me, the establishment of CAAM would give the body the freedom and opportunity to select and employ qualified technical officers to ensure that Malaysia's obligation in adhering to the safety of the national aviation industry is in line with the ICAO aspirations.

As mentioned above, the freedom to choose the most qualified officers to serve CAAM will be more beneficial if the CAAM can provide salaries and remunerations that are in line with that of local as well as the regional aviation industry.

Every civil aviation authority in the world will be audited by ICAO and other major regulatory bodies such as the US Federal Aviation Administration (FAA) and the European Aviation Safety Agency (EASA). The basis of the audit is to ensure that the civil aviation authority complies with the standards and recommended practices of ICAO.

The process of transforming the DCA to CAAM started in 2006 under the then Minister of Transport, Datuk Seri Chan Kong Choy. Thereafter, it went through four Ministers before it finally materialised in 2018 under the leadership of Datuk Seri Liow Tiong Lai.

Since I was one of the pioneer staff from in the initial transformation process, I am grateful to the Government for approving the transformation from DCA' to CAAM.

It is hope that the CAAM can take the nation's civil aviation industry to a greater heights.

Honoured with ICAO's Highest Recognition

ICAO is a UN agency responsible for the principles and policies of international air travel to ensure safe and orderly manner. Established in 1944, ICAO was formed to ensure a safer, more efficient, sustainable and competitive civil aviation sector.

An ICAO General Assembly is held every three years for a duration of two weeks. It is held at the ICAO Headquarters in Montreal, Canada, and attended by all the 193 Contracting States, 30 international aviation industry companies/bodies as well as Non-Governmental Organisations (NGOs) related to international civil aviation activities.

At the 39th ICAO General Assembly which took place in September 2016, I was elected as the President of the General Assembly. The said election represented one of the highest recognition in the world of civil aviation. It was a positive indicator of international support for the Malaysian leadership in civil aviation internationally, thus reflecting confidence in Malaysia's capability and achievement in this sector.

Furthermore, during the General Assembly, Malaysia regained its global credibility when it was re-elected as a Member of the ICAO

As the President of 39th ICAO General Assembly, September 2016.

A Special Plaque to commemorate the successful 39th ICAO General Assembly was immortalised at the ICAO Museum in Montreal.

At the closing of the 39th ICAO General Assembly with the President of ICAO, Dr. Aliu on the right and the Secretary General, Dr. Fang Liu on the left.

Council for the term of 2016–2019. Malaysia together with Singapore were the two ASEAN countries elected as the Members of the ICAO Council. Other countries elected to the Council from the Asia-Pacific region are China, India, Japan, Australia, and South Korea.

The election of Malaysia as ICAO Council Member for the fourth consecutive term since 2007 was a milestone for the country.

The most significant achievement of the 39th ICAO Assembly was its success in getting the ICAO Contracting States present to accept the proposal for the Carbon Offsetting and Reduction Scheme for International Aviation (CORSIA). The scheme was an effort to reduce carbon emissions in the international aviation sector to minimise the impact of climatic change.

The objective of the scheme was to protect the environment from climatic changes that could cause global warming. The melting of the ice in the Arctic Circle and the Antarctic Circle may result in rising sea levels causing small islands to sink and disappear from the surface of the earth.

Aviation is the leading transport sector in implementing and practising this scheme which is most important for the future of our earth.

In recognition of the ICAO resolution at the 39th General Assembly, a special plaque signifying the acceptance of the CORSIA proposal with a photograph of me as the President of the Assembly alongside Dr. Olumuyiwa Benard Aliu, the President of the ICAO Council, and Dr. Fang Liu, the Secretary-General of the ICAO, was immortalised at the ICAO Museum in Montreal.

I felt pride in my heart when I look at the picture on the plaque, feeling honoured that it brought recognition to Malaysia at the highest level in the international civil aviation forum.

Aviation has been a core part of my life since childhood
and
it will remain so for the rest of my life.

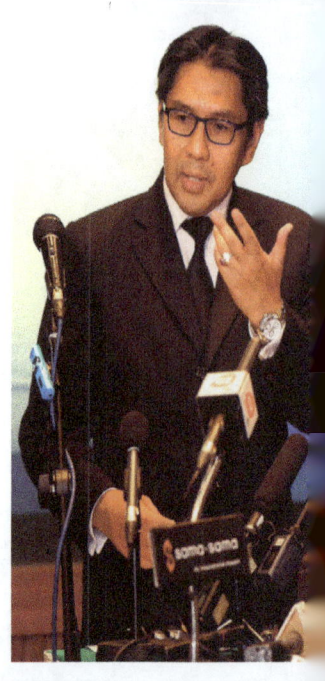

The List of Passengers

MH370 Passenger List

No.	Name	Country of Origin
1	An/Wenlan	China
2	Bao/Yuanhua	China
3	Bai/Xiaomo	Canada
4	Bian/Maoqin	China
5	Bian/Liangjing	China
6	Bibynazli/MohdHassim	Malaysia
7	Brodskii/Nikolai	Russia
8	Burrows/Rodney (Mr)	Australia
9	Burrows/Mary (Mrs)	Australia
10	Cao/Rui	China
11	Chan/Huanpeen (Mr)	Malaysia
12	Che/Juanzhang	China
13	Chen/Jian	China
14	Chen/Changjun (Mr)	China
15	Chen/Wei	Malaysia
16	Chen/Yun (Ms)	China
17	Chew/Karmooi (Ms)	Malaysia
18	Chuang/Hsiuling (Ms)	Taiwan

No.	Name	Country of Origin
19	Chng/Mei	Malaysia
20	Chustrak/Oleg	Ukraine
21	Dai/Shuling	China
22	Daisy/Anne	Malaysia
23	Deineka/Sergii	Ukraine
24	Di/Jiabin	China
25	Dina/MohamedYunusRamli	Malaysia
26	Ding/Ying	China
27	Ding/Lijun	China
28	Ding/Yingg (Ms)	China
29	Dong/Guowei	China
30	Dou/Yunshan (Mr)	China
31	Du/Wen	China
32	Feng/Dong	China
33	Feng/Jixin	China
34	Fu/Baofeng	China
35	Gan/Tao	China
36	Gan/Fuxiang	China
37	Gao/Ge	China
38	Gu/Naijun	Australia
39	Guan/Huajin (Ms)	Malaysia
40	Guan/Wenjie (Mr)	China
41	Han/Jing	China
42	Hashim/Noorida	Malaysia
43	Hou/Aiqin (Ms)	China
44	Hou/Bo	China
45	Hu/SiswanChd	China
46	Hu/Xiaoning (Mr)	China
47	Huang/Yi (Ms)	China
48	Huang/Tiuanhui	China
49	Hue/Puiheng (Mr)	Malaysia

No.	Name	Country of Origin
50	Jia/Ping	China
51	Jiang/Cuiyun	China
52	Jiang/Xueren	China
53	Jiang/Ying (Ms)	China
54	Jiao/Weiwei	China
55	Jiao/Wenxue	China
56	Jianghang/Jee	Malaysia
57	Ju/Kun	China
58	Kang/Xu	China
59	Koh/Tiongmeng	Malaysia
60	Kolekar/Chetana	India
61	Kolekar/Swanand	India
62	Kolekar/Vinod	India
63	Kozel/Christian	Austria
64	Lawton/Catherine (Mrs)	Australia
65	Lawton/Robert (Mr)	Australia
66	Lee/Kahkin (Mr)	Malaysia
67	Lee/Sewchu (Mdm)	Malaysia
68	Li/Yanlin	China
69	Li/Zhi	China
70	Li/Guohui	China
71	Li/Hongjing	China
72	Li/Jie	China
73	Li/Mingzhong	China
74	Li/Wenbo	China
75	Li/Yan	China
76	Li/Yuan	Australia
77	Li/Yuchen	China
78	Li/Zhijin	China
79	Li/Zhixin	China
80	Li/Le	China

No.	Name	Country of Origin
81	Liang/Luyang (Mr)	China
82	Liang/Xuyang	China
83	Lim/Powchua (Ms)	Malaysia
84	Lin/Annan (Mr)	China
85	Lin/Mingfeng	China
86	Liu/Fengying	China
87	Liu/Jinpeng (Mr)	China
88	Liu/Qiang	China
89	Liu/Rusheng	China
90	Liu/Shunchao	China
91	Liu/Zhongfu	China
92	Lou/Baotang	China
93	Lu/Jianhua	China
94	Lu/Xianchu	China
95	Lui/Ching	China
96	Luo/Wei	China
97	Ma/Wenzhi	China
98	Ma/Jun (Mr)	China
99	Maimaitijiang/A	China
100	Mao/Tugui	China
101	Maraldi/Luigi	Italy
102	Maria/MohamedYunusRamli	Malaysia
103	MatRahim/Norfadzillah (Miss)	Malaysia
104	Meng/NicoleChd	USA
105	Meng/Bing	China
106	Meng/Fanquan	China
107	Meng/Gaosheng	China
108	MohdKhairulAmri/Selamat (Mr)	Malaysia
109	MohamadSofuan/Ibrahim (Mr)	Malaysia
110	MuhammadRazahan/Zamani (Mr)	Malaysia
111	Mustafa/Suhaili (Miss)	Malaysia

The List of Passengers

No.	Name	Country of Origin
112	Mukherjee/Muktesh	Canada
113	Ng/Mayli (Ms)	Malaysia
114	Norliakmar/Hamid (Mdm)	Malaysia
115	Ouyang/Xin	China
116	Puspanathan/Subramaniam	Malaysia
117	Ramlan/Safuan (Mr)	Malaysia
118	Sharma/Chandrika (Ms)	India
119	Shi/Xianwen	China
120	Shirsath/Kranti	India
121	Sim/Kengwei	Malaysia
122	Siregar/Firman	India
123	Song/Feifei (Mr)	China
124	Song/Chunling (Ms)	China
125	Song/Kun	China
126	Su/Qiangguo	China
127	Suadaya/Ferryindra (Mr)	Indonesia
128	Suadaya/Herryindra (Mr)	Indonesia
129	Sugianto/Lo (Mr)	Indonesia
130	Surtidahlia (Mrs)	Netherlands
131	Tan/Teikhin (Mr)	Malaysia
132	Tan/Ahmeng (Mr)	Malaysia
133	Tan/Weichew (Mr)	Malaysia
134	Tan/Chongling	Malaysia
135	Tan/Sioh	Malaysia
136	Tang/Xudong	China
137	Tang/Xuezhu (Ms)	China
138	Tanurisam/Indrasuria (Mr)	Indonesia
139	Tee/Linkeong (Mr)	Malaysia
140	Teoh/Kimlun (Mr)	Malaysia
141	Tian/Junwei	China
142	Tian/Qingjun	China

No.	Name	Country of Origin
143	Tong/Sonlee (Mr)	Malaysia
144	Vinny/Chynthyatio (Mrs)	Indonesia
145	Wan/Hackkhoon (Mr)	Malaysia
146	Wang/Shouxian	China
147	Wang/Shu	China
148	Wang/Xianjun	China
149	Wang/Chunhua (Mr)	China
150	Wang/Chunyong	China
151	Wang/Dan	China
152	Wang/Haitao	China
153	Wang/Houbin	China
154	Wang/Linshi	China
155	Wang/Willysurijanto (Mr)	Indonesia
156	Wang/Yonggang (Mr)	China
157	Wang/Yonghui	China
158	Wang/Yongqiang	China
159	Wang/Lijun	China
160	Wang/Ximin	New Zealand
161	Wang/Rui	China
162	Wang/Moheng	China
163	Wattrelos/Ambre	France
164	Wattrelos/Hadrien	France
165	Wattrelos/Laurence	France
166	Weeks/Paul (Mr)	New Zealand
167	Wen/Yongsheng	China
168	Wen/Hao	China
169	Weng/Mei	China
170	Wong/Saisang (Mr)	Malaysia
171	Wood/Philip	USA
172	Xie/Liping	China
173	Xin/Xixi (Ms)	China

No.	Name	Country of Origin
174	Xing/FengTao	China
175	Xing/Qiao	China
176	Xiong/Deming	China
177	Xu/Chuane	China
178	Ya/Na	China
179	Yan/Ling (Mr)	China
180	Yan/Peng	China
181	Yan/Xiao	China
182	Yang/Li	China
183	Yang/Ailing (Ms)	China
184	Yang/Jiabao	China
185	Yang/Meihua	China
186	Yang/Qingyuan (Mr)	China
187	Yang/Xiaoming (Ms)	China
188	Yao/Jainfeng	China
189	Yao/Lifei	China
190	Yap/Cheemeng (Mr)	China
191	Yin/Boyan	China
192	Yin/Yuewang	China
193	Yuan/Jin	China
194	Yue/Guiju (Ms)	China
195	Yue/Wenchao	China
196	Yusop/Muzi (Mr)	Malaysia
197	Zang/Lingdi	China
198	Zhang/Chi	China
199	Zhang/Liqin	China
200	Zhang/Qi (Ms)	China
201	Zhang/Hua (Mr)	China
202	Zhang/Lijuan (Ms)	China
203	Zhang/Na (Ms)	China
204	Zhang/Siming	China

No.	Name	Country of Origin
205	Zhang/Xiaolei (Ms)	China
206	Zhang/Hualian	China
207	Zhang/Jianwu	China
208	Zhang/Jinquan	China
209	Zhang/Meng	China
210	Zhang/Xuewen (Mr)	China
211	Zhang/Yan	China
212	Zhang/Yan	China
213	Zhang/Yan	USA
214	Zhang/Yanhui	China
215	Zhang/Zhonghai	China
216	Zhang/Shaohua	China
217	Zhang/Gang (Mr)	China
218	Zhao/Qiwei (Mr)	China
219	Zhao/Yingxin (Chd)	China
220	Zhao/Peng	China
221	Zhao/Yan	France
222	Zhao/Zhaofang	China
223	Zheng/Ruixian	China
224	Zhao/Feng	China
225	Zhou/Jinling	China
226	Zhou/Shijie	China
227	Zhu/Junyan	China

MH370 List of Pilots and Cabin Crew

No.	Name
1	Zaharie Ahmad Shah (Captain/Pilot)
2	Fariq Ab Hamid (Co-Pilot)
3	Patrick Francis Gomes
4	Andrew Nari
5	Goh Sock Lay

No.	Name
6	Tan Ser Kuin
7	Wan Swaid Wan Ismail
8	Junaidi Mohd Kassim
9	Mohd Hazrin Mohamed Hasnan
10	Ng Yar Chien
11	Foong Wai Yueng
12	Tan Size Hiang

MH17 Passenger List

No.	Name	Country of Origin
1	Aafke Devries	Netherlands
2	Adinda Larasati Putri Vanmuijlwijk	Netherlands
3	Albert Rizk	Australia
4	Alex Ploeg	Netherlands
5	Allard Vankeulen	Netherlands
6	Amel Wals	Netherlands
7	Andre Anghel	Canada
8	Andrew Hoare	United Kingdom
9	Anelene Rostijem Misran	Netherlands
10	Angelique Gianotten	Netherlands
11	Annemieke Hakse	Netherlands
12	Annetje Dejong	Netherlands
13	Anthonius Vanveldhuizen	Netherlands
14	Anton Camfferman	Netherlands
15	April Vandoorn	Netherlands
16	Ariza Binti Gazalee	Malaysia
17	Arjen Ryder	Australia
18	Arnoud Huizen	Netherlands
19	Astrid Hornikx	Netherlands
20	Augustinus Moors	Netherlands
21	Auke Dalstra	Netherlands

No.	Name	Country of Origin
22	Barbaramaria Debruin	Netherlands
23	Barry Kooijmans	Netherlands
24	Benjamin Pocock	United Kingdom
25	Benoit Chardome	Belgium
26	Bente Vandermeer	Netherlands
27	Brett Wals	Netherlands
28	Bryce Fredriksz	Netherlands
29	Cameron Dalziel	United Kingdom
30	Carlijn Smallenburg	Netherlands
31	Carol Clancy	Australia
32	Caroline Vandoorn	Netherlands
33	Catharina Bras	Netherlands
34	Catharina Ruijter	Netherlands
35	Charles Eliza David Tamtelahitu	Netherlands
36	Charles Smallenburg	Netherlands
37	Christiene Desadeleer	Netherlands
38	Christina Anna Elisa Vandenschoo	Netherlands
39	Christopher Allen	Netherlands
40	Clarice Yelena Huizen	Indonesia
41	Cornelia Janssen	Netherlands
42	Cornelia Stuiver	Netherlands
43	Cornelia Tol	Netherlands
44	Cornelia Voorham	Netherlands
45	Cornelis Schilder	Netherlands
46	Dafne Nieveen	Netherlands
47	Daisy Oehlers	Netherlands
48	Daisy Risah	Netherlands
49	Darryl Gunawan	Philippines
50	Davy Joseph Gerardus Hally	Netherlands
51	Desiree Zantkuijl	Netherlands
52	Donny Toekiran Djodikromo	Netherlands

No.	Name	Country of Origin
53	Edel Mahady	Australia
54	Edith Cuijpers	Netherlands
55	Elaine Teoh	Malaysia
56	Eline Vranckx	Netherlands
57	Elisabeth Brouwers	Netherlands
58	Elizabeth Martens	Netherlands
59	Elsemiek Deborts	Netherlands
60	Emiel Mehler	Netherlands
61	Emile Vanmuijlwijk	Netherlands
62	Emma Bell	Australia
63	Emma Essers	Netherlands
64	Ericus Vanderpoel	Netherlands
65	Erik Peter Vanheijningen	Netherlands
66	Erik Vleesenbeek	Netherlands
67	Esther Deridder	Netherlands
68	Esther Dewaal	Netherlands
69	Evie Coco Anne Maslin	Australia
70	Fatima Dyczynski	Germany
71	Fleur Vandermeer	Netherlands
72	Francescam Davison	Australia
73	Frank Vanderweide	Netherlands
74	Frederique Vanzijtveld	Netherlands
75	Friso Hoare	Netherlands
76	Gabriele Lauschet	Germany
77	Gary Slok	Netherlands
78	Geertruida Heemskerk	Netherlands
79	Gerardus Menke	Netherlands
80	Gerardus Timmers	Netherlands
81	Gerda Leliana Lahenda	Indonesia
82	Gijsbert Vanduijn	Netherlands
83	Glenn Raymond Thomas	United Kingdom

No.	Name	Country of Origin
84	Hadiono Gunawan	Indonesia
85	Hannah Sophia Meuleman	Netherlands
86	Hasni Hardi Bin Parlan	Malaysia
87	Helen Borgsteede	Netherlands
88	Helena Sidelik	Australia
89	Hendrik Wagemans	Netherlands
90	Hendrikjan Tournier	Netherlands
91	Hendrikrokus Kroon	Netherlands
92	Hendry	Indonesia
93	Henricus Maas	Netherlands
94	Hielkje Raap	Netherlands
95	Howard Horder	Australia
96	Hubertus Lambregts	Netherlands
97	Huub Vanvreeswijk	Netherlands
98	Ian Allen	Netherlands
99	Ineke Westerveld	Netherlands
100	Inge Vandersar	Netherlands
101	Ingrid Meijer	Netherlands
102	Irene Gunawan	Philippines
103	Isa Kooijmans	Netherlands
104	Ithamar Avnon	Netherlands
105	Jack Samuel Obrien	Australia
106	Jacqueline Vantongeren	Netherlands
107	Jan Noreilde	Belgium
108	Jan Vandersteen	Netherlands
109	Jane M Adi Soetjipto	Indonesia
110	Jasper Hoare	Netherlands
111	Jennifer Vanderleij	United Kingdom
112	Jeroen Renkers	Netherlands
113	Jeroen Vankeulen	Netherlands
114	Jeroen Vendemortel	Netherlands

No.	Name	Country of Origin
115	Jeroen Wals	Netherlands
116	Jianhan Benjamin Lee	Malaysia
117	Jillhelen Guard	Australia
118	Jinte Wals	Netherlands
119	Johanna Dehaan	Netherlands
120	Johanna Nelissen	Netherlands
121	Johannes Lahaye	Netherlands
122	Johannes Rudolfus Vandenhende	Netherlands
123	John Alder	United Kingdom
124	John Allen	United Kingdom
125	Johnny Paulissen	Netherlands
126	Jolette Nuesink	Netherlands
127	Joopalbert Deroo	Netherlands
128	Joseph Lange	Netherlands
129	Joycemrs Baay	Netherlands
130	Julian Allen	Netherlands
131	Julian Ottochian	Netherlands
132	Kaelamayajay Goes	Malaysia
133	Karamjitsingh Karnailsingh	Malaysia
134	Karlijn Keijzer	Netherlands
135	Katharina Hoonakker	Netherlands
136	Kaushalya Jairamdas Punjabi	Malaysia
137	Ketut Wiartini	Indonesia
138	Kevin Jesurun	Netherlands
139	Kiah Yeen Lee	Malaysia
140	Kim Elisa Petronella Verhaegh	Netherlands
141	Klaas Willem Vanluik	Netherlands
142	Laurens Vandergraaff	Netherlands
143	Leonardus Wels	Netherlands
144	Liam Davison	Australia
145	Liam Sweeney	United Kingdom

No.	Name	Country of Origin
146	Lidwina Heerkens	Netherlands
147	Liliane Derden	Australia
148	Lisa Marckelbach	Netherlands
149	Lisanne Laura Engels	Netherlands
150	Liv Trugg	Netherlands
151	Lorenzo Vandekraats	Netherlands
152	Lubberta Palm	Netherlands
153	Luciepaulamaria Vanmens	Netherlands
154	Lyetielisabeth Ng	Malaysia
155	Maarten Devos	Netherlands
156	Mabel Anthonysamy	Malaysia
157	Marco Grippeling	Netherlands
158	Maree Rizk	Australia
159	Margaux Larissa Vandenhende	Netherlands
160	Maria Smolders	Netherlands
161	Mariaadriana Deschutter	Netherlands
162	Mariam Huntjens	Netherlands
163	Marie Vermeulen	Netherlands
164	Marit Witteveen	Netherlands
165	Mark Vanderlinde	Netherlands
166	Marnix Reduan Vandenhende	Netherlands
167	Marsha Azmeena Binti Tambi	Malaysia
168	Martin Paulissen	Netherlands
169	Mary Menke	New Zealand
170	Mary Tiernan	Australia
171	Mattheus Kamsma	Netherlands
172	Mathew Ezekial Sivagnanam	Malaysia
173	Megan Hally	Netherlands
174	Melinganak Mula	Malaysia
175	Merel Vanderlinde	Netherlands
176	Michael Clancy	Australia

No.	Name	Country of Origin
177	Miguel G Panduwinata	Netherlands
178	Milia Vandemortel	Netherlands
179	Ming Lee Foo	Malaysia
180	Minhchau Dang	Netherlands
181	Mira Kooijmans	Netherlands
182	Mo Robert Anderson Maslin	Australia
183	Mohd Ali Bin Md Salim	Malaysia
184	Mona Chens Sim Lee	Australia
185	Muhammad Afif Tambi	Malaysia
186	Muhammad Afruz Bin Tambi	Malaysia
187	Muhammad Afzal Bin Tambi	Malaysia
188	Natashja Binda	Netherlands
189	Ngoc Minh Nguyen	Netherlands
190	Nicoll Charles Anderson Norris	Australia
191	Ninik Yuriani	Indonesia
192	Olga Ioppa	Germany
193	Oscar Kotte	Netherlands
194	Otis Samuel Frederick Maslin	Australia
195	Paul Goes	Netherlands
196	Paul Rajasingam Sivagnanam	Malaysia
197	Paulus Vandersande	Netherlands
198	Peter Essers	Netherlands
199	Peter Souren	Netherlands
200	Petra Vanlangeveld	Netherlands
201	Petronella Vaneldijk	Netherlands
202	Piers Adnan Vandenhende	Netherlands
203	Pieter Jan Willem Huijbers	Netherlands
204	Pijke Vanveldhuizen	Netherlands
205	Pim Wilhelm Dekuijer	Netherlands
206	Qingzheng Ng	Malaysia
207	Qium Kamsma	Netherlands

No.	Name	Country of Origin
208	Quinn Schansman	Netherlands
209	Quint Vanveldhuizen	Netherlands
210	Quocduy Dang	Netherlands
211	Rahimmah Noor	Malaysia
212	Regis Crolla	Netherlands
213	Reinmar Specken	Netherlands
214	Remco Kotte	Netherlands
215	Remco Trugg	Netherlands
216	Rene Vangeene	Netherlands
217	Richard Mayne	United Kingdom
218	Rik Schuyesmans	Belgium
219	Rishi Jhinkoe	Netherlands
220	Robert Ayley	United Kingdom
221	Robert Ploeg	Netherlands
222	Robert Vanderlinde	Netherlands
223	Robert Vankeulen	Netherlands
224	Robertjan Vandekraats	Netherlands
225	Robertjan Vanzijtveld	Netherlands
226	Robin Hemelrijk	Netherlands
227	Rogerwatson Guard	Australia
228	Rowen Bats	Netherlands
229	Sandra Martens	Netherlands
230	Sascha Meijer	Netherlands
231	Saskia Deleeuw	Netherlands
232	Sem Wels	Netherlands
233	Sergio Ottochian	Netherlands
234	Shaka T Panduwinata	Netherlands
235	Shaliza Zaini Dewa	Malaysia
236	Sherryl Gunawan	Philippines
237	Shiing Ng	Malaysia
238	Shun Po Fan	Netherlands

No.	Name	Country of Origin
239	Siew Poh Tan	Malaysia
240	Siti Amirah Binti Parawira	Malaysia
241	Sjors Adrianus Pijnenburg	Netherlands
242	Solenn Wals	Netherlands
243	Sophie Vandermeer	Netherlands
244	Sri Paulissen	Netherlands
245	Stefan F W Vannielen	Netherlands
246	Stephen Leslie Anderson	United Kingdom
247	Steven Noreilde	Belgium
248	Steven Vandersande	Netherlands
249	Subashni Jretnam	Malaysia
250	Supartini	Indonesia
251	Susan Hijmans	Netherlands
252	Susan Horder	Australia
253	Tallander Franciscus Niewold	Netherlands
254	Tamara Ernst	Netherlands
255	Tambi Bin Jiee	Malaysia
256	Tess Trugg	Netherlands
257	Tessa Vandersande	Netherlands
258	Thamsanqa Uijterlinde	Netherlands
259	Theresa Baker	Australia
260	Therese Brouwer	Netherlands
261	Tim Nieburg	Netherlands
262	Tim Renkers	Netherlands
263	Tina Pauline Mastenbroek	Netherlands
264	Valentijn Essers	Netherlands
265	Vickiline Kurniati Kardia	Indonesia
266	Victor Oreshkin	Australia
267	Wayan Sujana	Indonesia
268	Wayne Baker	Australia
269	Werther Smallenburg	Netherlands

No.	Name	Country of Origin
270	Why Keong Lee	Australia
271	Wilhelminalouise Broghammer	Germany
272	Wilhelmus Grootscholten	Netherlands
273	Willem Bakker	Netherlands
274	Willem Witteveen	Netherlands
275	Winneke Vanwiggen	Netherlands
276	Wouter Vorsselman	Netherlands
277	Yanhwa Loh	Netherlands
278	Yau Chee Liew	Malaysia
279	Yodricunda Theistiasih	Indonesia
280	Yuli Hastini	Indonesia
281	Yvonne Kappen	Netherlands
282	Yvonne Ryder	Australia
283	Zeger Leonard Vanheijningen	Netherlands

MH17 List of Pilots and Cabin Crew

No.	Name
1	Wan Amran Wan Hussin (Captain/Pilot)
2	Eugene Choo Jin Leong (Captain/Pilot)
3	Ahmad Hakimi Hanapi (Co-Pilot)
4	Muhamad Firdaus Abdul Rahim (Co-Pilot)
5	Mohd Ghafar Abu Bakar
6	Dora Shahila binti Kassim
7	Azrina binti Yakob
8	Lee Hui Pin
9	Mastura Mustafa
10	Chong Yee Pheng
11	Shaikh Mohd Noor Mahmood
12	Sanjid Singh Sandhu
13	Hamfazlin Sham Mohamed Arifin
14	Nur Shazana Mohamed Salleh
15	Angeline Premila Rajandara

Index

A
accusations, 127–128
Acting Minister of Transport, 5, 13, 17, 80–81
Air Accidents Investigation Branch (AAIB), 15–17, 20–22, 29, 33, 71, 77, 100–101, 119–120, 126
Air New Zealand (ANZ), xxii–xxiii
Air Traffic Control Centre (ATCC), 6–7
Air Traffic Control Tower (ATC), 7, 63
Air Transport Safety Board (ATSB), 22
Aircraft Communications and Reporting System (ACARS), 11, 131
Aman, Anifah, 102
AN-26 transport aeroplane, 135
Andaman Sea, 28
Annex 13, 21–22, 59, 104–105, 125, 138
Attorney General Chambers (AGC), 69
Attorney General Chambers of Malaysia, 41, 70
Australia Transport Safety Board (ATSB), 34
Autonomous Underwater Vehicles (AUV), 48, 55

B
bathymetric survey, 34, 37
Bay of Bengal, 28–29
Belgian Air Force, 100
black boxes, 34, 54, 61, 67–68, 98–101, 107, 119–123, 127–128
Boeing 777, 6, 15, 22, 72, 95, 137
British Council, xx
British Council Library, xx
Bureau d'Enquetes et d'Analyses (BEA), 22, 69–70

C
Carbon Offsetting and Reduction Scheme for International Aviation (CORSIA), 150
CASA, 73
Certificate of Release, xxv
Chartered Institute of Transport (CIT), xxvi
China, 59, 83–84, 91
Civil Aviation Authority (CAA), xxv

Civil Aviation Authority of China (CAAC), 22
Civil Aviation Authority of Malaysia (CAAM), 7, 146–147
Clifford Primary School, xvi–xvii, 17
Cockpit Voice Recorder (CVR), 54, 63, 68, 100, 119–120
Commonwealth Scientific and Industry Research Organisation (CSIRO), 77
conspiracy theories, 59–60, 134–135
Counter Terrorism Investigation Department, 70
Cranfield Institute of Technology (CIT), xxvii
criminal investigation, 125
Crisis Media Centre, 135

D

DCA Operations Centre, 113
Defence Science and Technology (DST), 77
Department of Civil Aviation (DCA), xi, xiii, xv–xxvii, 7, 10, 16, 34, 48, 51, 80, 95, 104, 111, 114, 129, 143
Diego Garcia, 64
Director-General of DCA, 4
Directors-General of Customs, 75
Disaster Victim Identification (DVI), 108–109
Dnipropetrovsk Air Traffic Controller, 120
drift search area, 42–43
drift simulation, 43
Dutch, 47, 104, 108, 117, 126, 137
Dutch Public Prosecution Service, 137
Dutch Safety Board (DSB), 104, 126

E

European Aviation Safety Agency (EASA), 147

F

Federal Aviation Administration (FAA), 147
Final Investigation Report, 104, 127, 137–139
flaperon, 68, 70–74
Flight Data Recorder (FDR), 54, 63, 100, 121
Flight Information Region (FIR), 6–7
forensic investigation, 125–128
France, 70–74
French Judiciary, 69–70
Fugro search operations, 39

G

14th General Elections, 56–58
Government-to-Government's (G2G) Domestic Clearance, 27

H

HCM ATCC, 7–10
Head of the Investigation Team, 67
High-Level Technical Task Force (HLTTF), 11, 13–14, 41, 46, 85
Ho Chi Minh, 6
Hussein, Hishammuddin, 81

I

Indian Ocean, 16–23, 33–34, 44, 64, 68, 87
Inmarsat satellite, 11–12, 16–18, 29, 33–34, 41, 77
international air traffic management, 60

International Civil Aviation Organization (ICAO), xxvi, 6–8, 13, 100, 131, 138, 146–150
International Court of Justice (ICJ), 117

J
Jauhari, Ahmad, 5
Joint Agency Coordination Centre (JACC), 33
Joint Investigation Team (JIT), 105, 117, 126, 135

K
Kampung Maxwell, xviii
KL Air Traffic Control Centre (KL ATCC), 7–9
Kota Kinabalu FIR (KK FIR), 7
Kuala Lumpur, xvii–xix, xx–xxi, 21, 85, 97, 145
Kuala Lumpur Aeronautical Rescue Coordination Centre, 9
Kuala Lumpur International Airport (KLIA), 3–4, 6, 62, 74, 97, 101, 114
Kuching Air Traffic Control Centre, 7

L
Letter of Agreement (LOA), 8, 10
Licenced Aircraft Maintenance Engineer (LAME), xxv
Lincoln Library, xx

M
9M-MRO, 6, 138
Malaysia Airlines System (MAS), xix–xxi, 5, 13, 64, 72, 80, 130–132
Malaysia Airports Holdings Berhad (MAHB), 5
Malaysia Certificate of Education (MCE), xix
Malaysia's reputation, 130–132
Malaysian Ambassador to France, 70
Malaysian Cabinet, 23
Malaysian Government, 34, 45–46, 57, 65, 70, 76, 84, 87, 91, 98, 101, 117, 122, 128, 131, 134
Malaysian Investigation Team, 123
Malaysian Maritime Enforcement Agency (MMEA), 27
Malaysian team, 100, 108, 111–114
MAS B777, 4, 18, 51
MAS Operations Centre, 97
MASkargo, 64
MAS-MARA Training Programme, xxi
Maxwell School, xviii
media, 79–86, 129–132
Member of the Chartered Institute of Transport (MCIT), xxvi
Memorandums of Understanding (MOU), xxii, 22
MH17, xii, 95–150
MH370, 3–23, 25–86
MH370 debris, 76–77
MH370 Safety Investigation Team, 67
Mindanao, 65–66
Ministry of Defence, 47
Ministry of Health, 89
Ministry of Health Malaysia (MOH), 111
Ministry of Transport (MOT), 5, 51, 67, 75, 101, 130–131
Minister of Transport Malaysia, 96
MV Fugro Equator, 47
Mysterious Cargo, 64–65

N

9N314M-model, 123, 127, 134, 137
National Transport Safety Board (NTSB), 11, 22, 71
Netherlands Government, 101
New Zealand, xxii–xxiv
Non-Governmental Organisations (NGOs), 134, 148
Nordin, Abdul Halim Ahmad, 47
Northern Corridor, 25, 29–32

O

Ocean Infinity, 45–51, 53–54, 56–57, 78
Omar, Ismail, 70
Organization for Security and Cooperation in Europe (OSCE), 102

P

Pakatan Harapan, 57
People's Republic of China (PRC), 83
Philippines, 65–66
pilot, xvi, xix, xx, xxv, 10, 61, 63, 103
psychic, 84–86
Public Security Bureau of China, 59
Public Service Department, xxvii
Putin, Vladimir, 122

Q

Quality Control Committee, 110
Quran, 86

R

Real-Time Aircraft Tracking, 131
remote control, MH370 Hijacked via, 61–63
Remote Underwater Vehicle (RUV), 54
repatriation process, 107–108
Rescue Coordination Center (RCC), 27

Rosedee, Azmi, 47
Royal Malaysia Police (RMP), 14, 65
Royal Malaysian Air Force (RMAF), xv, 10, 15, 114
Royal Malaysian Navy, 47
Royal Malaysian Police (RMP), 111
Russia, 105, 127, 129, 135
Russia-Ukraine border, 96

S

Sakri, Mohd, 98–99
Santa Secondary School, xvi–xvii
satellite communication (SATCOM), 77
Seabed Constructor, 47, 54–55
Search and Rescue (SAR) operation, 5, 14–15, 27, 34
search areas, 12, 15, 27–28, 33–38, 41–42, 48, 50, 52, 58, 78
search operations, 11, 13, 15, 21–22, 25, 27–28, 33–34, 39–41, 44, 47–49, 52–54, 56, 77, 81, 83–84, 96, 131–132
Search Strategy Working Group (SSWG), 32–34, 77
Shaman, 79–86
social media theories, 133–134
South China Sea (SCS), 27–29
South Corridor, 29–32
Southern Corridor, 17–18, 20, 25, 29
southern Indian Ocean, 17, 19–21, 23, 33, 47, 88
SQ351, 123
Standard Operating Procedure (SOP), 20
Straits of Malacca, 28

T

Tamilian's Physical Cultural Association (TCPA), xviii
Tanzania, 75–76
Tebuan jet, xvi

technical investigation, 125
The Dozen Persons, 34
The Malaysian ICAO Annex 13 Safety Investigation Team for MH370, 13–14
tragedy, 95–105
Trainee Aircraft Maintenance Engineer (TAME), xxii
Training Course in Aircraft Maintenance, xxii
Transition Phase, 34
transponder, 11

U
Ukraine, 96–97, 100–101, 121, 123, 125–127, 129, 135
Ukraine's Air Traffic Control, 96
Ukrainian Ministry of Foreign Affairs, 127
underwater search, 27, 37–38, 40
United Nations (UN), 99

V
victims, 110–111, 115–116

W
waypoint BITOD, 10
waypoint IGARI, 6–15, 27
waypoint RND, 120
waypoint TAMAK, 96
waypoint TIKNA, 120

Y
Yusof, Md Noor, 101

www.ingramcontent.com/pod-product-compliance
Lightning Source LLC
Chambersburg PA
CBHW061940220426
43662CB00012B/1972